Larissa Babij

A Kind of Refugee

The Story of an American Who Refused to Leave Ukraine

With a foreword by Vladislav Davidzon

UKRAINIAN VOICES

Collected by Andreas Umland

The book series "Ukrainian Voices" publishes English- and German-language monographs, edited volumes, document collections, and anthologies of articles authored and composed by Ukrainian politicians, intellectuals, activists, officials, researchers, and diplomats. The series' aim is to introduce Western and other audiences to Ukrainian explorations, deliberations and interpretations of historic and current, domestic, and international affairs. The purpose of these books is to make non-Ukrainian readers familiar with how some prominent Ukrainians approach, view and assess their country's development and position in the world. The series was founded, and the volumes are collected by Andreas Umland, Dr. phil. (FU Berlin), Ph. D. (Cambridge), Associate Professor of Politics at the Kyiv-Mohyla Academy and an Analyst in the Stockholm Centre for Eastern European Studies at the Swedish Institute of International Affairs.

Larissa Babij

A KIND OF REFUGEE

The Story of an American
Who Refused to Leave Ukraine

With a foreword by Vladislav Davidzon

Bibliographic information published by the Deutsche Nationalbibliothek
Die Deutsche Nationalbibliothek lists this publication in the Deutsche
Nationalbibliografie; detailed bibliographic data are available in the Internet at
http://dnb.d-nb.de.

Bibliografische Information der Deutschen Nationalbibliothek
Die Deutsche Nationalbibliothek verzeichnet diese Publikation in der Deutschen Nationalbibliografie;
detaillierte bibliografische Daten sind im Internet über http://dnb.d-nb.de abrufbar.

Cover picture: View of the Kyiv skyline from the author's window, May 2022.
Photo by Larissa Babij

Map design: Iryna Derii
Illustrations: Lisa Biletska

ISBN-13: 978-3-8382-1898-4
© *ibidem*-Verlag, Hannover • Stuttgart 2024
All rights reserved.

Printed in the United States of America

To my grandmothers
"Busia" Irena and "Babtsia" Maria

Contents

Contents

Foreword
By Vladislav Davidzon

I am an American, Chicago born—Chicago, that somber city—and go at things
as I have taught myself, free-style, and will make the record in my own way: first
to knock, first admitted; sometimes an innocent knock, sometimes a not so innocent. But a man's character is his fate, says Heraclitus, and in the end there isn't
any way to disguise the nature of the knocks by acoustical work on the door or
gloving the knuckles.
—Saul Bellow, *The Adventures of Augie March*

Larissa Babij is Ukrainian, American born in Manchester, Connecticut, which despite its historic silk factories was dully suburban.
Like Augie March she would make her own idiosyncratic way and
record, freestyle—recursively returning to her ancestral lands.
Abandoning the new world for the old, Babij would send the word
back to the new. Thus spake Bellow of the character of the hero in
Heraclitus—his point being, perhaps, that ultimately every such
hero is a priori a critic. The book that you are holding in your hands,
A Kind of Refugee, is a collection of writings that first began as wartime dispatches and occasional salvos to concerned friends and relatives. They are—as the reader will doubtless find—absolutely
gripping. This book constitutes an important addition to the literature of primary documents and diaries recounting the first year of
the full-scale war that Russia liberally unleashed in Ukraine in 2022.
It offers—from the pen of a literate and fluid Ukrainian-cultured
native writer of English—one of the very best and most humane
accounts of what we felt and experienced during those first months
of unspeakable violence.

Larissa and I were first introduced in 2017, in the eastern
Ukrainian city of Kharkiv (once the capital of the Ukrainian Soviet
republic) by a mutual friend. That friend was Yevgeniy Fiks, a
Russian-born American artist whom I knew from my New York
days, with whom Babij had co-curated the exhibition "In Edenia, a
City of the Future," featuring an international group of renowned
contemporary artists. The exhibition at the Yermilov Art Center
took its name and inspiration from Yiddish author Kalman

Zingman's 1918 utopian novella, which was published in Kharkiv in the midst of the Russian Empire's dissolution into revolution and war; the short-lived Ukrainian republic's declaration of national autonomy for Jews, Russians, and Poles; and the looming establishment of a Bolshevik Communist USSR. The Yiddish writer's work prophesied an idealistic, multicultural, and futurist fantasia of ethnic comity (a worthy precedent for the cultural activists—of whom Babij was one—who were working to reshape Ukraine, after the 2013-2014 Maidan protests, into a vibrant political nation).

Zingman's novel was set in the far-off future of 1943, which— as we all now know—would not turn out to be a year particularly renowned for its spirit of liberal ethnic comity. That same year, incidentally, Babij's Ukrainian grandparents would have to abandon their homes in the country's west, setting them on the path to becoming refugees. The exhibition sparked viewers to meditate on utopia—whether with forlorn nostalgia or with the vision of a dream curdled into a nightmare. Larissa and I would eventually become close friends—may all of your own friends, dear reader, be as generous and loyal in that art form as is Babij.

Larissa's path is noteworthy in that she left her original Ukrainian diaspora habitat to return to the land of her ancestors. Her depiction of the fabric of daily life as an ordinary citizen in wartime Ukraine is as deeply felt as it is intelligent. Unsurprisingly for a dancer and performer, Babij channels and processes information through her body. Her sensibility is syncretic—at once cerebral, sensual, and poetic.

Babij is also a culture worker par excellence: she has engaged in writing, translating, editing, curating, criticism, and teaching over nearly two decades in Ukraine. She was one of the most valued editorial staff members of the literary journal *The Odessa Review*, which I edited together with my wife Regina Maryanovska-Davidzon in the years after the Maidan. In February 2014, when the Maidan revolution succeeded in removing Ukraine's authoritarian presidential administration from power (and the war began with Russia's insidious invasion of Crimea), Babij and other change-oriented culture workers occupied the basement of the Ministry of Culture. Their protest against that monument of ossified Soviet stagnation was a distillation of the values of the Maidan. That "pragmatically utopian" attempt to liquidate the ministry has yet to achieve its goal.

When Babij posits that she is "a Kind of Refugee," this is a characteristically thoughtful and wry assertion. The sobriquet intimates that there exists a wide variety and great teeming typology of refugees. Long before she was forced to abandon her Kyiv apartment by the rain of Russian missiles and approaching tanks and troops, her grandparents had been refugees after World War II. Two of them spent time in the limbo of a DP (displaced persons) camp, while two made their own way through chaotic postwar Europe — all of them eventually making it to immigrant heaven. That is, to America. Growing up in Connecticut, Larissa was faced with the traditional choice demanded by American assimilation — to embrace or to efface. Ukraine would pull her back. This book is written from the perspective of an eternal insider outsider, and Babij is continually reliving her grandparents' displacement. Doing so, she has a deep sense that to be a Ukrainian (even one who was born into the comforts of North American life) is to understand how all present-day Ukrainians bear deep scars of intergenerational trauma. Indeed, her thoughtful reflections on what her grandparents lived through form the narrative spine of the book and constitute its moral and historical core. Her epistles, which offer a sense of the extraordinary recent past, are as remarkably astute as they are clever and witty.

It should be noted that Babij's background is in Ukrainian avant-garde theater. And she writes about it from a historically literate perspective, being one of Ukraine's most sensitive and penetrating theater critics. Her writing is always lyrical, passionate, and convincing. Some of her long-form theater criticism appeared in the culture section of *The Odessa Review* (and nothing makes an editor more thrilled than to publish a critic of her acuity and powers of observation). Her later interest in the Feldenkrais method, a movement practice that fosters a holistic recognition of the connections between the mind and body, should come as no surprise. It is part and parcel of her commitment to understanding reality and history through the movements of the body.

A Kind of Refugee is very much redolent of Larissa's real life spirit and voice. The text is suffused with what we routinely think of as particularly American traits—warm openness, directness, curiosity, nonjudgmental generosity, and gumption. The story is related in the unadorned and colloquial register of thought, and her effervescent positivity can be felt everywhere throughout the work. Reading Larissa's charged epistles from Mykolaiv or Lviv or her home in Kyiv, it is obvious that one is in the presence of a historically aware, sensitive, and canny observer of the textures of social relations and everyday life. If Babij also observes that the Ukrainians are not a philosophical nation—as opposed to other European nations who have contributed greatly to the history of Western philosophy—she means that Ukrainians are more practical and action-oriented. Perhaps certain historical conditions are necessary for a nation to develop an inclination to philosophize. Could centuries of repression and suffering dull the capacity for thought? Larissa Babij's first book categorically negates that thesis. While serving as an excellent guide to these horrific times, it is a deeply important work of philosophic candor and observation by an incredibly perceptive critic.

Introduction

It is summer 2023 and I am at home in Kyiv. Ukraine has been at war against Russia's unilateral full-scale invasion for over 500 days. Really, the invasion began in 2014, when Russia sent its "little green men" to take over Ukraine's Crimean Peninsula. Now darkness has violently flooded into the heart of Europe, threatening to extinguish the life of the Ukrainian nation. It will keep expanding its reach as long as it is allowed.

This book is an invitation to revisit the recent past, when Russia was bombing Ukrainian civilians sheltering in their own cities, attacking evacuation corridors, striking public squares in bustling daytime hours with missiles, and committing war crimes in Ukraine. Remember Russia's contemptuous and cynical motivations for its violations of international law? What about your own agitation while following the news of the war and wondering how Ukrainians were fighting and surviving? I remember Western people emanating an impervious confidence that they ultimately have everything under control, no matter their position toward Ukraine or the suffering of its people. And I remember having the distinct sense that the outcome of the war depends on what I do.

I no longer remember what it feels like for the power to go out unexpectedly when I'm in the middle of replying to an email; or how the air in my apartment feels at 12°C; or the newness of sounds of explosions (intentional military ones) several blocks away. Recalling the most difficult and darkest moments of your history requires working against your own nature, which favors the recollection of pleasant sensations. The past is always in danger of receding into darkness (from where it threatens to take over the future). But I should not need to be an active participant in a 21st-century war to begin to make sense of what my grandparents endured during World War II. I should not need to be the target of enemy missiles to discover my own power to fight against evil. What did you and I — and all of us together — not learn from the history of the 20th century?

Life is sharper and vision more acute when pressed up against death. This is a story of approaching the past through present-day experience. It is also a story of being swept up in historic events without getting carried away. It is a testament to the power of adhering to what is important to you without knowing what's going to happen next. War puts you face-to-face with decisions that affect more than your personal well-being and survival. Your actions and decisions drive the further course of events and the destiny of your grandchildren, your country, and the whole world.

***

I grew up in the United States in the late 20th century, the grandchild of Ukrainians who left their homes under life-threatening pressure during World War II. My parents, sister, and I lived in a house in the suburbs with a yard, two cars, and a pet cat. My grandparents presided over holidays, babysat when my parents went out, and saved money to send their grandchildren to prestigious US universities.

My grandmother "Busya" Irena lived to be 92; "Babtsya" Maria has made it past 96. I got to know them in their kitchens. The culture of their homeland seeped into me through the language we spoke, through the smells and flavors of their respective borschts, through the rituals of weekly church-going, obedience, and reverence for one's elders.

When Babtsya Maria and I made traditional Easter bread in her kitchen, I'd ask about her life before. How many times, while kneading dough, did I hear the story about the group of young people, a mix of Poles and Ukrainians, who moved west through Germany after the war, looking for food and medical care, while avoiding the Soviet authorities looking to "repatriate" their citizens? Maria got married in a displaced persons (DP) camp at age 19. Her dress was made of parachute silk.

Disparate images and incomplete stories offered glimpses into a world that had no analogue in the suburban US approaching the turn of the millennium. I was vexed by the sense that I knew something deep in my bones, cells, psyche—let's call it the experience of war—which I could not have learned in my immediate surroundings.

My grandparents came from Halychyna, a region in Ukraine's west that was ruled by Austria-Hungary, then Poland. When the Soviets invaded in 1939, Maria was a 12-year-old schoolgirl in a rural village. Irena, a schoolteacher, was married and pregnant with her first child. Two years later, the Nazis arrived. In 1943, they took all the able-bodied youth from Maria's village to Germany as forced laborers. That year Irena's husband was targeted for assassination by Polish insurgents, and the couple fled westward with their young son. I will never know what my grandparents experienced during those abrupt departures and in the turbulent war years before my parents were born.[1] But I can say from experience that war changes you irreversibly.

The vibrant Ukrainian diaspora community provided a living connection to a lost world I had never seen. My childhood was a kaleidoscope of activities aimed at keeping my Ukrainian heritage alive: Saturday school, church, scouts, folk dancing . . . The community largely comprised post-WWII immigrants, many of whom had passed through the DP camps[2] (which had their own lively cultural and educational life). Relationships forged in wartime intensity were renewed on the North American continent; my grandparents also maintained lifelong friendships with Ukrainians who'd resettled in Australia and England. The Ukrainian diaspora was committed to preserving the language, culture, and identity of its homeland, which was being ruthlessly plundered and suppressed by the Communist Soviet regime. We took great pride in this mission.

---

1   My parents were born in Europe just after the war. They grew up in the US as immigrants and met decades later at a Ukrainian diaspora New Year's dance.

2   After the war, Europe was flooded with displaced persons (DPs), including millions from regions of Eastern Europe that by 1945 were controlled by the Soviet Union. The USSR was eager to repatriate the people it claimed as its citizens, especially Ukrainians. Hundreds of thousands of repatriates were executed upon arrival in the USSR and over 2 million were sent to labor camps, where only half of those imprisoned survived their terms. This was punishment for the alleged crime of aiding the Nazis, no matter that millions of these "assistants" were taken to Germany by force (as Ostarbeiters) or as prisoners of war. Some DPs chose suicide over returning to the Soviet "motherland." See https://www.encyclopediaofukraine.com/display.asp?linkpath=pages%5CR%5CCE%5CRepatriation.htm.

Membership in this community — with its language and traditions and the ephemeral knowledge of mass violence — made me strange in the eyes of my American classmates. My family spoke Ukrainian, a language my neighbors told me was the same as Russian. We celebrated Christmas Eve with twelve dishes with untranslatable names that were nothing like American cuisine. At Ukrainian scout camp we would sing around the bonfire. Images of dashing Cossack freedom fighters helping maidens hoist water from the well emanated romance through lyric verses set to haunting melodies. But at home I got my water from the tap, and the guys in my high school were busy playing video games.

My grandparents were hard-working and self-reliant in a way that seemed redundant in the consumer culture of the late 20th-century US. Poring through clothing, furniture, and travel catalogues, I'd imagine myself inhabiting the scenes on every page. But there was a disconnect between me and all that glittering promise. Sensing that the Hollywood movies I watched could tell me nothing about my grandparents' wartime experience, I began to doubt whether I could trust that the world around me was real. But the colorful lands of the folk songs I loved were also a fantasy world, detached from the cars and wall-to-wall carpets that were indisputably present in the American suburbs.

The dream of Ukraine's independence from the Soviet Union became reality in 1991, when I was 11 years old. It happened without bloodshed. On August 24, Ukraine's parliament declared independence, and in December it was ratified by nationwide referendum, with support from over 90% of the country's population.

The land of stories and songs that I had grown up imagining was now a country with the world's third-largest nuclear arsenal and a population whose savings became worthless overnight. When my family visited Ukraine in 1997, as we walked through the village where my relatives lived, the kids picked ripe plums off the dirt road, wiped them off, and ate them. Gross! Driving between cities, we passed endless fields of sunflowers, just as I had imagined, and billboards advertising Coca-Cola — which complicated my romantic vision of Ukraine.

My best friends in college in New York City were Russian Jews who had emigrated just after the USSR collapsed. It was awkward when I invited them home for Ukrainian holidays. My grandparents remembered the Russians as mortal enemies (and were casually disdainful of Jews), but I was determined to see past old prejudices – we were all American compatriots now. By that time I was aware of the enormous gap between the imaginary Ukraine I had grown to love through my patriotic diaspora upbringing and the actual present-day post-Soviet country Ukraine, which I knew next to nothing about.

***

In 2005, on a wave of optimism after the 2004 Orange Revolution, I arrived in Ukraine's capital Kyiv, curious and clueless. It was the summer after some one million Ukrainians had demonstrated on Kyiv's central Independence Square (Maidan Nezalezhnosti) in sub-freezing temperatures to protest the results of a rigged presidential election. The non-violent protesters demanded a re-vote to ensure a fair chance for opposition candidate Viktor Yushchenko, who had been poisoned by his Kremlin-friendly opponent in the run-up, which permanently disfigured his face. Yushchenko represented a Europe- and NATO-oriented course for Ukraine, in contrast to the previous administration's support for the Kremlin and its methods for eliminating opposition.[3] Ukraine's Supreme Court ordered another election – this time, closely monitored by domestic and international observers – where Yushchenko won by a significant margin.

---

3   In 2000, while Leonid Kuchma was president, Georgiy Gongadze, a Ukrainian journalist known for investigating government corruption and for championing free speech, was kidnapped and murdered. While the murder investigation ordered by the president stalled, tape recordings surfaced that implicated Kuchma in the journalist's disappearance, sparking mass protests in the center of Kyiv (December 2000–March 2001) demanding his resignation. Kuchma served out his term until 2004, but did not succeed in getting his chosen successor into office. He has never been officially charged in relation to Gongadze's murder. In 2014 and 2015, he served as Ukraine's representative in the Trilateral Contact Group that signed the Minsk agreements.

Fourteen years independent, Ukraine was a teenager. To me it seemed like there was so much space for building, for transformation, for contributing to the construction of a new democratic society. Yushchenko's presidency, colored by inflated expectations and constant infighting within the administration, was too chaotic even for the change-oriented public that elected him. In 2010, disappointed and yearning for stability, in a moment where life is stranger than fiction, Ukrainians legitimately elected Yushchenko's former opponent Viktor Yanukovych[4] to the highest office. Through democratic procedure, Ukrainians chose the stability and familiarity of a government that would rule through repression, corruption, and pleasing the Kremlin, with its members primarily working to increase their personal wealth. Freedom, after all, is insecure, unpredictable, and ultimately uncomfortable.

I spent those years living in Kyiv, working with the experimental performing artists of TanzLaboratorium and immersing myself in the ferment of the budding contemporary art scene—first as a translator, then reviewing exhibitions, then working together with the artists to organize public events, exhibitions, and publications. Working in the contemporary arts in Ukraine, with its entrenched Soviet legacy of art serving the reigning ideology (enshrined in the Ministry of Culture), involved reimagining the infrastructure to support our art. This meant reforming existing institutions, experimenting with forms of working together, and making our work visible in the international art world. Activism just went with the territory.

So when journalist Mustafa Nayyem wrote his famous Facebook post[5] on November 21, 2013, calling all Ukrainians who cared about their country's future and were dismayed about President

---

4   Yanukovych, originally selected to succeed Kuchma, was known for his criminal background in his native Donetsk region and for his pro-Russian foreign policy. His public image and campaign were shaped by a savvy American political consultant named Paul J. Manafort, who would later manage Donald Trump's campaign for US president. In 2017 Manafort was indicted in the US probe into Russian interference in the 2016 election.

5   At the time Afghani-Ukrainian Mustafa Nayyem was an investigative journalist and activist. He ended his post calling for people to come to Maidan with the phrase: "Likes don't count."

Yanukovych's refusal to sign an association agreement between Ukraine and the EU to go to Kyiv's central square, I headed for Maidan Nezalezhnosti. Most Ukrainians, especially the younger generations, imagined their future in Europe and felt betrayed by the president's abrupt shift of the national course toward Russia. The modest demonstrations continued until the night of November 30, when riot police were ordered to clear the square; they violently attacked the protesters, mostly students, injuring dozens. The following day, several hundred thousand people filled the center of Kyiv to protest their government's abuse of police power and brutality toward its citizens. By the winter of 2013–2014 it was time to grow up.

The dramatic and deadly Maidan protests (also known as the Revolution of Dignity) were live-streamed, so people around the world watched in real time as a mass of black-suited riot police pressed in on the crowd on the night of December 10. People kept coming from all over Ukraine to the center of Kyiv: for three winter months Maidan was crowded with tents, movement, and arguments. Warming themselves around fires in oil drums on the street, people who had previously never crossed paths began to discuss their visions of the country they wanted to live in. Refusing to cower before the government's threats, Ukrainian protesters positioned themselves in public space to demand that the country's politicians respect and serve the citizens' political needs.

By February 20, 2014, regime-friendly and Kremlin-backed snipers had killed around a hundred protesters. These deaths were recorded on camera, and the protesters' funerals were broadcast too. Only Yanukovych's abdication and flight to Russia the following evening happened in the shadows. Ukrainians succeeded in ousting their corrupt, authoritarian government, which was subservient to Russia, and demonstrated to the world that they were ready to fight and shed blood to make their country their own.

Then in late February, "little green men" (Russian forces in military gear, but without insignia) appeared in Ukraine's autonomous republic of Crimea, quietly launching Russia's invasion that continues to this day. In March, people who spoke Russian with a different accent than the locals appeared on the streets of Donetsk and in other cities in Ukraine's eastern regions. The "separatist" movement, fomented by Russia and bolstered by the participation of Russian citizens,[6] used violent force to take over local government buildings across Ukraine's Donetsk and Luhansk regions and proclaim the establishment of "people's republics."

The Ukrainian government declared an anti-terrorist operation (ATO) to reclaim its cities and lands. Many of the protesters that had come to Kyiv's Maidan immediately went east, becoming the volunteer forces fighting the undeclared Russian invasion and supplying those forces with whatever they could. In 2014, Ukraine's official military had just over a hundred thousand troops, having grown feeble during the years since independence.[7] The interim government hastily reinstated the National Guard and called on regional governments to form and equip battalions to bolster Ukraine's armed forces. Bloody battles, fought largely by volunteer battalions equipped by Ukrainian businessmen and civic activists, continued intensely through 2015.

Ukraine's present-day valiant defense is rooted in this early trial by fire. Many members of the Armed Forces who hold leadership roles today received their combat education in the ATO's first years — in lessons learned through huge losses. Ukrainians' success in ousting their pro-Russian government in 2014 gives power and legitimacy to their ongoing fight against Russian domination.

***

Maidan remained occupied until August 2014. The activists who remained in Kyiv formed groups aimed at government oversight and policy reform. In fall 2014 I bought an apartment in Kyiv. My commitment was to artistic reflection, institutional reform in culture, and supporting my Ukrainian colleagues who understood that at the heart of the violent conflict that had materialized in

---

6   https://kyivindependent.com/the-origins-of-the-2014-war-in-donbas/.

7   After 1991, Ukraine pursued a course of nuclear disarmament (transferring the arsenal it inherited after the collapse of the USSR to Russia); flirted with forms of military alliance with other former Soviet republics; and — under Yanukovych — adopted non-aligned status.

Ukraine's east lay the unresolved question of how contemporary Ukraine must deal with its Soviet past.

It was not enough for Ukrainians to claim to be victims of the Communist party of the USSR, even when Soviet policy had intentionally killed millions of Ukrainians (for instance, in the 1932–1933 Holodomor famine, and in the purges of artistic and intellectual elites that climaxed in 1937). A victim is always in need of an aggressor. Ukrainians had to acknowledge and account for their own instrumental participation in establishing the USSR in 1922, in the latter's systemic murder of tens of millions of its own citizens, through to its 1991 collapse. Artists whose brilliance we celebrate today — like Ukrainian theater director Les Kurbas, who was executed by the Soviet regime in 1937 — were intimately involved in building the Soviet Ukrainian state, where arts and ideology were deeply entwined.

By 2014, addressing the Soviet legacy in Ukrainian art production had left the realm of theoretical debate. In the basement of the Ministry of Culture, now occupied by culture activists, we practiced group decision-making via assembly and called for the liquidation of the outdated institute that reproduced a Soviet approach to culture in independent Ukraine. The Ministry was good for supporting corruption schemes and imitating artistic activity, but terrible for encouraging the production of innovative, thought-provoking culture that would invite, encourage, and inspire audiences to think independently.

Here I was, an American-born and -educated translator and art curator, in a room full of Soviet- and Ukrainian-born artists and activists. Energized by the Maidan protests and driven by the urgency of the sudden Russian invasion, we were trying to rebuild an entire system. We had to change Ukraine. But we couldn't even discuss a concept like "institution" without understanding where an institution comes from. This meant beginning to address our vastly different political backgrounds. And learning how to speak to one another.

Finding myself trying to collectively draft a national cultural policy with my Ukrainian colleagues — none of us with appropriate professional qualifications, but each sensing the immediate need for change—I got a taste of how much hard work democracy really requires. This was nothing like what I had learned growing up in the US, where it was clear what avenues were available for citizen participation. The rules and traditions for voicing your opinion were set, along with who has the authority to make decisions in the large machine that seemed to run mostly on its own inertia.

***

In March of 2014, just after Russia invaded Crimea, the senator from my home state met privately with a handful of American citizens in Kyiv. He and his aide were just a bit older than me. All of us were scarred by the experience of the US's reckless invasion of Iraq in 2003 under the false pretext that the country was harboring weapons of mass destruction. The American officials were clear: we do not want to repeat the experience of entering into an overseas war that we later regret.

But what about historical responsibility? In 1994, the US—together with the UK and Russia—signed the Budapest Memorandum, welcoming the accession of Ukraine to the Nuclear Non-Proliferation Treaty. The document obliged the signatories to refrain from threat or use of force against the territorial integrity or political independence of Ukraine. In fact the US had pressed Ukraine to give up the nuclear arms it inherited after the fall of the USSR—to Russia!

Twenty years later, in 2014, Russia had outright invaded Ukraine's Crimean Peninsula and annexed it illegally while the other Budapest Memorandum signatories looked on uncomfortably. The US imposed sanctions on a dozen individuals associated with the Russian government and the EU followed suit. It took over a week following the Russian Federation's illegal annexation of Crimea for the United Nations General Assembly to adopt a resolution "calling on States, international organizations and specialized agencies not to recognize any change in the status of Crimea or the Black Sea port city of Sevastopol."[8] It also called on states (as if

---

8   https://press.un.org/en/2014/ga11493.doc.htm.

retroactively) to "desist and refrain from actions aimed at disrupting Ukraine's national unity and territorial integrity, including by modifying its borders through the threat or use of force."[9]

This was the beginning of the West's murky Ukraine policy of mixing indignant speech with ultimate appeasement of Russia. No UN member state was willing to act decisively — politically or militarily — to stop Russia from taking whatever pieces of Ukraine that it wanted, as long as Ukraine was unable to withstand such incursions.

***

With Crimea and the eastern regions of Ukraine now de facto controlled by Russia or its proxies, the people who lived there had to decide with whom they belonged. Ukrainian citizens, such as filmmaker turned political prisoner Oleh Sentsov,[10] faced persecution and the threat of unlawful detention in their home cities, simply for their pro-Ukrainian political position. The Indigenous Crimean Tatars have been subject to systematic repression and human rights abuses, leading the activist and current political prisoner Nariman Dzhelal to compare Crimea to "a concentration camp."[11] In Donetsk, the occupation authorities turned the Izolyatsia contemporary art center into a prison camp, where they imprisoned Stanislav Aseyev, who had reported on life in the "DPR" using a pen name. Just acting like a free citizen of Ukraine was not allowed by the new "authorities."

Parts of Ukraine — which millions of Ukrainian citizens had called home — were now a territory with an ambiguous status — neither fully under Ukrainian government control, nor self-governing as their declared "people's republic" names would suggest, nor

---

9   Ibid.
10   Oleh Sentsov was arrested in his native Simferopol, Crimea, by Russian authorities in May 2014. Detained on false charges, he was taken to Russia and in 2015 was sentenced by a Russian court to 20 years in prison. His unlawful imprisonment, during which he went on a hunger strike, garnered worldwide attention. He was released in a prisoner swap and returned to Ukraine in 2019. As of 2023, he was fighting in the Armed Forces of Ukraine.
11   https://www.pravda.com.ua/eng/articles/2022/02/27/7326286/.

de jure ruled by Russia though de facto that was close to the truth. Kyiv and other cities throughout Ukraine began filling with internally displaced persons (IDPs). A promising contemporary dancer from Donetsk became my roommate. She made a point of speaking Ukrainian in public; established an innovative dance school for kids in Kyiv; and periodically, unbeknownst to me, suffered debilitating panic attacks. The people who had fled or fought against Russian occupation faced the challenge of assimilating into communities where the war seemed distant. New government programs and international funding initiatives were launched in Ukraine to provide support to IDPs and veterans of the ATO. Meanwhile Ukrainians and the world at large were beginning to assimilate the idea that a sizable swath of the country was now an obscure region beyond the pale of international agreements or law or justice.

Minsk I, Minsk II, and the "contact line" separating the eastern regions of Ukraine into government-controlled and non-government-controlled territory stabilized.[12] By 2016, the fighting in the east looked like a "frozen conflict," with a few Ukrainian soldiers being killed each day but no shifts in territorial control. Russian forces, still claiming to be "separatists," refused to move their military equipment and continued to shoot across the contact line at Ukrainian soldiers. These soldiers, under orders not to return fire (as required by the Minsk agreements), remained in position to

---

12   The Minsk agreements, drafted by the Trilateral Contact Group on Ukraine (with one representative each from Ukraine, Russia, and the Organization for Security and Cooperation in Europe – and mediated by the leaders of France and Germany), were signed in September 2014 and February 2015. The leaders of the self-proclaimed and internationally unrecognized "Donetsk People's Republic" and "Luhansk People's Republic" also signed the documents without being parties to the agreement. The measures to be implemented included an immediate ceasefire; withdrawal of heavy weapons and the creation of a demilitarized security zone; release of all hostages and prisoners; restoration of state border control to the Ukrainian government; pullout of all foreign armed formations and military equipment; and alteration of Ukraine's constitution to grant special status to particular areas of the Donetsk and Luhansk regions. Russia maintained that it was not a party to the agreements, and they were never implemented in full by either side. See also Duncan Allan's 2020 analysis in "The Minsk Conundrum": https://www.chathamhouse.org/2020/05/minsk-conundrum-western-policy-and-russias-war-eastern-ukraine.

protect their country, while people in their country, living further from the contact line, began to adjust to the status quo.

***

In this context of legalized ambiguity I began studying the Feldenkrais Method of somatic education. Learning to listen to my physical sensations in movement; to discern the difference between what I am really doing and what I want to be doing; and to direct the movement of my attention was a profoundly therapeutic gift. I spent a few years traveling between the US and Kyiv, attending professional Feldenkrais teacher training sessions several times a year in New York City.

In Ukraine there was a growing need to help combat veterans transition to civilian life and to help people from the country's war-torn eastern regions recover from or continue living with the stress of ongoing shelling from Russia-backed separatists. Letting go of unnecessary physical tension, learning to regulate how much effort you put into a task, reminding your body of its natural rhythms — all this can be very helpful for people in situations of extreme stress or who have lived through traumatic experiences. I translated for American somatics practitioners training Ukrainian psychologists and social workers whose clients — and often they themselves — lived close to the contact line between Ukrainian and non-government-controlled territory. We practiced ways of encouraging people to turn more attention to their physical sensations, to their breath, to where they are in space.

Moshe Feldenkrais, who invented the method I was studying, reminded his students, "We cannot function satisfactorily if our thinking, senses, and feelings do not affect our acts or responses."[13] It sounds like common sense. But I was so accustomed to making decisions based on what I imagined might happen or what I thought others expected from me that this was a revelation.

Beginning to rediscover and repair the connections between my own sensing, feeling, thinking, and doing seemed like a

---

13   Moshe Feldenkrais, *The Elusive Obvious*, 1981, p. 37.

prerequisite to genuine participation in political life. After years of activism directed toward Ukrainian cultural institutions, I could not ignore my responsibility for the consequences of myself and my American compatriots taking democracy for granted for decades. Meanwhile Ukrainians—still entangled in their Soviet heritage—were constructing their democracy from the ground up in the midst of an undeclared Russian invasion. When I started teaching "Awareness Through Movement" classes based on the Feldenkrais Method, I thought helping people learn to sense what they were actually doing—as opposed to what they thought or hoped they were doing—might help prepare individuals for taking responsibility for their democracies.

Well, you have to start with yourself.

***

Living abroad gives you a vantage point from which to see the culture that has formed you. If I came to Ukraine drawn by a desire to encounter that precious quality that my grandparents were so heartbroken to leave behind, then in Ukraine I learned to see and value the firm principles upon which American democracy was founded (hard to see beneath the contentious jockeying that substitutes for American political life today). Ukrainians showed me through their gaze that I walk through the world with a sense of freedom as given, the gift of my American upbringing.

At the end of 2021, I took a trip to the US to visit family. There was no question that I would return to Ukraine for New Year's Eve as planned, despite the Russian troops massing ominously at Ukraine's borders. I had a dance to go to. I had learned to dance the Lindy Hop in Kyiv and joined the vibrant local community of swing dancers who cherished big band jazz music. Growing up in the US, I'd gone to zabavas—social dances with live bands organized by Ukrainian diaspora communities—where we'd dance the polka and the waltz and a simplified tango, sharing the dance floor with our grandparents. Communities sustain our connection to those who came before us and to those who will follow. They're enlivened by those who are present, while holding space for those who aren't.

Home is more than the apartment where I sleep and wash and eat and work. It's the city of Kyiv, where I often run into people I know, even if we haven't spoken in years. And it is the invisible web of personal relationships, built upon hours and years of my life shared with specific people over the decades. My communities today are not organized or founded on identity (how we name ourselves or what other people call us) but through doing things together and through repeated encounters. Being seen, recognized, receiving affirmation that you exist in somebody else's vision is incredibly nourishing and perhaps necessary to feel like a human being. These chance encounters — a sign that when each of us is doing our own thing, our actions, interests, and principles still bring us to the same place — tell me I am home.

By mid-February 2022, US citizens like me were being urged to leave Ukraine. I'd heard numerous public statements, received emails from the US State Department, and even gotten a personal phone call. My Ukrainian friends were carrying on undaunted. We'd been at war for eight years already. Unwilling to flee preemptively, I wrote a Facebook post expressing my commitment to staying in my home city of Kyiv: "There is a certain power in standing your ground. There is certainly power in exercising your own wits, intuition and curiosity; while giving up the basic (and ever-challenging) practice of standing up for what's yours is a pretty sure path to capitulation."

I had no idea what was coming.

***

After Russia invaded Ukraine full-force on February 24, 2022, sending a hundred cruise missiles into cities around the country, I received a flood of messages from people abroad — close friends and family and people I hadn't spoken to in decades who remembered I'm Ukrainian and suddenly found me on the Internet. There was no time to answer every single one individually to assure them that I am, if not exactly safe, then okay.

So during an air raid alarm, soon after I arrived in Lviv in late February, I began writing my first letter as "a kind of refugee" to everyone abroad who might care.[14] Each of the dispatches in this book was written under pressure, while sleep-deprived, in between countless other urgent activities, and sent off right away. War forces you to be strict with priorities: whatever you don't do now may forever remain undone. You have no idea what the next hour (let alone tomorrow) may bring, so better pull yourself together and write it and post it now. That way, your message will be out in the world and publicly accessible, no matter where you will be.

The situation around me was changing, and with every event, with every challenge met, with every devastating blow, I too was changing. At first I was just fleeing, surviving, doing what needed to be done in response to a situation that was continuously new (and terrifying). But then my mind started to change. I started to see and realize things. Tiredness sets in. You get used to living under attack, surviving your own decisions, enduring the losses wrought by war and as a result of your own decisions. I don't know exactly what is happening to me as I am transformed by the war.

I've edited my dispatches only lightly (for the sake of clarity), adding footnotes where additional information is needed. Sometimes the letters refer to current events that would have been clear to readers following the news in the moment. I've added "scene summaries" describing some of what was going on in Ukraine as I was writing these letters (with no intention of producing a comprehensive chronicle of the war's events). The talented Lisa Biletska, Ukrainian artist and writer, made illustrations from my personal photos.

The book concludes with three essays on theater in Ukraine that I published between 2015 and 2018. The Ukrainian artists with whom I consorted then, particularly the performers of TanzLaboratorium, profoundly influenced how I think about politics, civic

---

14   The letters collected in this book were first published in real time on Substack, where I continue to post dispatches from Ukraine at war at "a Kind of Refugee." See akindofrefugee2022.substack.com.

responsibility, and the power each person has to shape the world we all live in.

***

Today's war is being played out in real time in view of the entire world.

Should it be a surprise that Ukraine's president Zelensky, a comedian and actor by profession, has stepped up to the task of leading his country and being the visible figurehead of a millions-strong citizen resistance? In performance—and comedians know this best—timing matters. In war it means the difference between success and failure, between life and death.

Military people and performers know that your life (the authenticity of your art) depends on what you pay attention to and on what you do. That will define the unpredictable situation you are in. You don't sit there wishing everything were different. You look and assess, you step in, you send out different kinds of signals, and you see what the response is. And *you* decide whether or not to engage and how and when to shift your approach. The performer, the fighter, or the mature adult knows that you always have several possibilities for action. There is an art in the choosing—and only after the fact can you begin to see more fully what that choice meant.

When the US government offered to evacuate Zelensky from Kyiv, as Russian forces quickly headed for the capital after February 24, he responded, "I need ammunition, not a ride." We remember his words only because he stayed, together with millions of Ukrainians who took up arms to defend Ukraine from the advancing Russian army.

I am still in Ukraine, writing from my apartment in Kyiv. As the grandchild of immigrants forced to leave their homeland under duress, I used to think that you are formed by what happens to you. After living in a country that's been at war for nearly 10 years, I've realized that you are formed by *how you respond* to what happens to you.

No person—or political nation—is wholly formed or completely doomed as long as they are alive. The decisions that ordinary people make every day—the way they respond to what happens to them—change or reinforce the structures of the world we share. Ukrainians are waging war against the Soviet system, while Russia is fighting to perpetuate that system's power throughout the world. Democratic citizens know that only your action and speech—your direct, messy participation—can keep the system from controlling you. Ukraine's spirited resistance, which means nothing without the simultaneous efforts of Ukrainians to build sturdy political structures to protect their own lives, proves that it is still possible today to act on principle, and that in your principles lies your power.

A Kind of Refugee:
A Journey through Ukraine at War,
in Three Acts

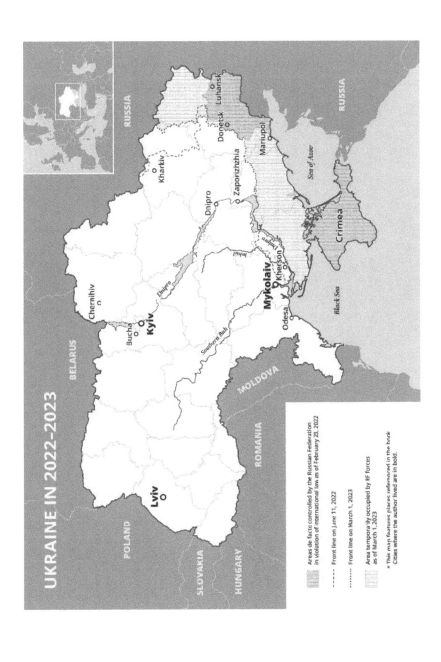

UKRAINE IN 2022-2023

RUSSIA

RUSSIA

BELARUS

POLAND

SLOVAKIA

HUNGARY

MOLDOVA

ROMANIA

Crimea

Sea of Azov

Black Sea

Luhansk

Donetsk

Mariupol

Kharkiv

Zaporizhzhia

Dnipro

Kherson

Mykolaiv

Odesa

Chernihiv

Bucha

Kyiv

Lviv

Dnipro

Southern Buh

Dnipro

Inhul

Inhulets

Areas de facto controlled by the Russian Federation in violation of international law as of February 23, 2022

Front line on June 11, 2022

Front line on March 1, 2023

Area temporarily occupied by RF forces as of March 1, 2023

* This map features places referenced in the book. Cities where the author lived are in bold.

Prologue

December 31, 2022, Kyiv

Drinking coffee in Kyiv, my friend the physical therapist says we all have PTSD. I've never been a fan of diagnoses. This is both a gift and a fault.

It's warm at home and the lights are on. No words can describe how tired I am.

On Monday I met a soldier who had shrapnel lodged in many parts of his body for a couple months while he was a prisoner of war. The pieces were surgically removed only after he returned to Ukraine in the fall.

Sitting in a cafe I marvel at this tall young man, still underweight, with bright, intelligent eyes. He came in on his own two legs; it's the third day he's walking unassisted. After the explosion that filled his body with shards of metal and glass he could only move his head.

"What did you do to get from that state to this?" I ask in wonder, watching his hands and fingers move lightly, same as anybody else's.

We talk about how the body naturally repels foreign objects; small pieces of metal or glass would gradually migrate toward the surface of his skin. "And you pulled them out with your fingers?" Yes, he says, and smiles.

***

My grandmother is missing the nail on one of her big toes—the result of an infection that appeared just after the war. She was moving westward through Germany to avoid Soviet forced repatriation, sleeping in fields and dirty vacated barracks, eating old potatoes or whatever her band of young traveling companions could scavenge. It was becoming too painful to walk when she happened upon a doctor who had the instruments to remove the infected part of her toe.

35

Growing up in the US, I was hungry for stories from the war. I yearned to understand what it was like, what happened there. What did people go through that afterward they were so reluctant to talk about? All they told me — with utter conviction — was, "May you never have to see what I did."

***

There is a threshold between comfortable, clean, civilized life and the brutality of war. From the vantage point of the former, the border may seem solid, even permanent. Anyone who has crossed it by chance knows that it can be shattered in an instant.

I remember the woman from Mariupol who agreed to be interviewed for French television in March, just after arriving at the train station in Lviv. Her willingness to talk and her insistence hinted that she was well off. Hanna was a lawyer, now bound for Bali after spending three weeks in a dark basement as her city was bombed relentlessly by the Russians. Deprived of light, they were afraid they would go blind. She had a message for the Red Cross and every international body: "Use your influence to get people out of Mariupol. These people want to live!"

Tens of thousands of Mariupol's residents have died. Those that remain in the city are wintering in apartments whose shattered windows are covered in flimsy plastic. The occupying Russian forces are renovating the Drama Theater that they bombed in the spring, killing hundreds who were sheltering inside. We will never know exactly how many people died in the city or what they experienced before their deaths.

***

Thursday morning I took a cab to a doctor's appointment, chatting excitedly with everyone I met — we were all a bit on edge following Russia's missile attack. By afternoon I've already forgotten about the four explosions I heard in the morning.

When the body is constantly at the mercy of the environment, whether this means protecting yourself from Russian strikes or catching the light to have a warm shower, you enter a state of being more agitated and alert, quick to speak and act, impatient of the dull softness that is the privilege of living in a country protected by a nuclear arsenal.

This kind of physical knowledge changes you, even if you still remember how to act civilized. You might blend right in but nobody knows where you've been, and even if you try to say it in words they understand, they remain on that side of an invisible wall and your excruciating job is to be a translator.

One gets used to living in inconsistency, to not being able to depend on anything or anybody. I feel changes in temperature, tiredness, anger. Not much else. But if the soldier I met could recover his movement enough to step onto the fast-moving escalator of the Kyiv metro, I'm sure I'll regain the ability to feel when it becomes relevant again.

***

A person flees from a war zone dirty, smelly, terrified. And then you wash them, feed them, give them a clean, warm place to sleep. And they still have the war with them. Everything they lived through.

A woman at a weekly support group for IDPs shares: "I don't like that I hate. I don't like that they have made us hate."

When my grandparents despised the Russians it wasn't through prejudice. It was a judgment based on experience.

Is the wish to permanently secure the wall protecting the sheltered life of civilization from the horrors of war a desire to remain innocent? To protect oneself from sharing the hardships that others have endured? To shield oneself from one's own darkness and ugliness?

Perhaps our great error (or crime) is succumbing to the illusion that the civilized world can be contained, sealing off the cracks through which people could slip out to scout the dangerous unruly territories beyond and return, taking it all in so that there is no longer an outside. And so the war starts to happen here, on the territory of the civilized world.

Act I

Scene 1

On February 24, 2022, the Russian Federation (RF) launches its full-scale invasion of Ukraine, minutes after its president called for neighboring Ukraine's "demilitarization and de-Nazification" in a televised broadcast. By 5 AM Russian cruise missiles are exploding around Kyiv, Kharkiv, Dnipro, Odesa, and other Ukrainian cities. Russian troops and military vehicles enter Ukraine from the east, north (via Belarus), and south (from occupied Crimea).

The Ukrainian army mounts a fierce defense and Ukraine's Jewish president, Volodymyr Zelensky, declares martial law. Hundreds of thousands of citizens sign up to join the resistance.

I flee westward from my home in Kyiv, eventually finding refuge in Lviv.

While Russian forces lay siege to Chernihiv, Kherson, and Mariupol; mercilessly shell Kharkiv; and press on the capital city Kyiv, Ukrainians from all over the country flood into Lviv. I connect with an activist friend and Ukrainian veterans to help supply military units and embattled hospitals, relying on my large international network of friends, family, and colleagues. I quickly realize that telling people outside Ukraine about what Russia's assault really looks like is no less important.

March 2, 2022, Lviv

I am writing this from the corridor as the air raid siren wails for the third time today. Luckily, although we hear sirens every day, the city of Lviv has not been hit by bombs or shelling (so far).

You're receiving this letter because we've been in touch in the past week and I want to share some moments and thoughts from my new life as a "kind of" refugee in Lviv: at once safe from the barbaric destruction of Ukraine's other cities and torn from the fabric of my former life in Kyiv, which now belongs to the past.

I fled the city I consider home the day Russia sent cruise missiles to targets all over Ukraine, the day I was awakened by a phone call at 5 AM from a friend asking, "Did you hear the explosions?" No, I didn't. And even after my ears heard the next ones, my stubborn mind refused to believe that the area around my beloved, fragile little apartment was being exploded by rockets that had flown through the air from neighboring Russia.

My friends and I (a motley group of three cats and five people) got into a car that afternoon and headed west. It took us two days to reach Lviv. Other friends took a principled stance to stay (especially those who had to abandon their homes in Donetsk eight years ago—finding themselves in Ukraine and having found Ukraine in themselves, now they are not budging).

Tonight will be my fourth night sleeping in the same place. It's been great for my cat, Telepatia, although every day she walks up to the door meowing with urgency, as if beyond that door she would find her old home. She is also constantly trying to jump/crawl/climb UP. Do cats have a sense of vertical equilibrium by which they feel their distance from the ground at all times? We used to live on the seventh floor, but now we are on the third.

I've joined a band of local volunteers (including old friends-colleagues from Lviv and some plucky recent arrivals) that is helping to organize the shipment and delivery of medical supplies from abroad to those who need it most in Ukraine, providing regular news updates for friends and journalists from around the world, and supporting recently arrived refugees, whether they are staying or moving further west toward Europe. I also now have seven pairs of underwear!

Countless friends, including artist colleagues I have not spoken to in years, have invited me to Bialystok, Lodz, Berlin, and even offered to drive to the Ukrainian border to pick me up. Thank you, friends: I do not want to leave Ukraine. This quandary between fleeing and standing—I've somehow managed to do both—is something I want to think through and, if you don't mind, share with you.

The decision to flee for protection or to stand your ground where you are is the primary existential question of the moment. The next question—addressed to any and all who stay—is what are you standing for? If in peacetime staying put can be a passive "choice," then war turns it into an act.

Today my heart is most with those still living in Kyiv, Kharkiv, and Mariupol, and with the Ukrainian armed forces and newly formed territorial defense battalions who are on the ground defending our cities and infrastructure from this unconscionable Russian brutality.

Glory to Ukraine! Death to the enemies!

March 6, 2022, Lviv

It is night. And deeply quiet. I am waiting for my old friend from Kyiv to arrive at my apartment. Yes, I am already calling it mine although I should remember that it is not.

Humans' capacity to adapt is incredible. I am already at home in war.

In the midst of war, people are still exactly who they are, only everything is intensified. Decisions must be made in light-seconds. I've passed through this state before, the one where your body is flooded with adrenaline, your thinking is unusually clear, your actions well-timed. It is the state before an approaching deadline, when all hands are on deck, when you have to defeat the distractions of fear/anxiety or laziness/sleep, those habits of mind that prevent you from performing superhuman feats. It is usually temporary, but now I am living in it.

The day after Sasha went back to Kyiv I was awoken by a phone call from Yuri, who had just arrived with his wife and her mother. Thirty-six hours later Yulia and Tatiana were in a car bound for Warsaw and I offered a place to Viktor, who appeared in our volunteer headquarters, and now Alisa is here too. I have met so many new people in the past week: Ivan, Katya, Zhenya, Karina, Nastya, Ulyana, Teimur . . .

The fabric of human connections that held me in place in Kyiv was ruptured the instant we all began to scatter. The friends I used to see and sense and touch on a regular basis are now in Kolomiya, Zakarpattia, Warsaw, Kyiv, and I don't know where. You can't see the destruction of this fabric of social bonds (fluid and subtle) like you can a gaping hole with charred edges in a building or a distant fire spewing black smoke. But it is no less devastating.

You still need human contact, and there is no time to build up those connections over repeated encounters and years. You are just open and available to every person you cross paths with. Whoever is right beside you is your partner in whatever you are doing and needing in this moment. Every person who is not the enemy is a friend, a compatriot, an ally.

Humans have a special sense with which they can tell almost immediately whether a person is of their environment, like if they belong to this city, if they are a part of its fabric. I used to take pride in being able to "pass" for a local when visiting a city and tourists would ask me for directions. But I was playing then.

This city is filling up with refugees. We look at each other as we pass on the street, sizing each other up and asking with our eyes, "Are you one of us?" It's a shy gaze and one that does not want to look too deep lest it be intrusive. Not only so as not to be disrespectful, but also because I'm not particularly ready to take in your pain too.

Today I spoke to my grandmother in Connecticut, the one whom I failed to call on her 95th birthday on February 24, though I was well aware of the coincidence as my friends and I made our way, point by point, further west from home. Our conversation is usually primitive. The repetitive questions serve as channels for a communication of love and attention that means more than the words. It's been years since we've talked about current world events.

Today she asked me something new: she asked if I had a problem.

"No," I said, "I am okay," discursively separating myself from the theater of war, to assure her of my safety (old habit).

"Don't go to the problem," she said.

"No," I responded, "no need, it will come by itself."

I understood then that she understands that I am on her path again. And I'm beginning to understand her story so much better from the inside.

My genetic inheritance has prepared me for this. And isn't that sad? "Sad"?! Can you find a word adequate to describe the fact that some 80 years after my grandmother was taken by the Nazis (those Nazis, the original ones) from her village in the west of the Lviv region to be a forced laborer on a farm in Germany and then she was a DP[15] and then a refugee, here I am? I realized decisively around February 20 that I do not want to be a refugee. Been there,

---

15   A Displaced Person. When World War II ended, Europe was flooded with people who had fled or had been forcibly removed from their homelands. DPs were largely Eastern European peoples who refused to return to their homes that had come under Soviet rule. Two of my grandparents, who had been forced laborers in Germany during the war, met and married in a DP camp.

done that.[16] "I" have been pushed out and away from my home once before. In some way, holding my ground in Lviv as an American citizen, I am with those people from Donetsk who refuse to leave the capital of Ukraine.

---

16   It's as if I inherited my grandparents' experience of fleeing their homeland. I felt like I had done it myself.

March 11, 2022, Lviv

This war has so many fronts, as many as there are places or dimensions, real and virtual, that I inhabit. Finding time to sleep is hard.

There were three or four quiet days. I even forgot how the air raid siren sounds. But the body remembers and was ready to move at its 5 AM call; it went off again after 11. Russian missiles destroyed the airports outside Ivano-Frankivsk and Lutsk this morning. Three missiles hit residential buildings and obliterated a shoe factory in Dnipro.

I'm sure you don't need me as a news source, but this is what I think about now. And learning new words and expressions—in Ukrainian and English—to describe what is going on here, like "Russia's brutal assault on Ukraine."

The constant activity on so many fronts also stimulates invention. I recently coined a new word in Ukrainian: післязараз. Resembling післязавтра (after tomorrow), it means "after now." When there are 5–10 things you need to attend to immediately and someone asks you for something, you say you'll do it післязараз.

March 16, 2022, Lviv

Today is Wednesday, March 16, 2022.

Twenty-one days since Russia launched 100 cruise missiles to begin its current assault of Ukraine (and 8 years, 24 days since Russia invaded Ukraine in the 21st century with the whole world witnessing).

Twenty-one days since I left my home in Kyiv, 19 since I arrived in Lviv, 18 that I've been living in this apartment. Since then, at various times, 6 other people have lived here; now we are 3.

Now 6 of my close friends are in Kyiv: 2 have joined the territorial defense of Kyiv; 1 is working as a fixer with 2 foreign journalists; 2 are training their puppy that they got in mid-February; 1 is a civilian fighting valiantly in the discursive war.

I have 2 pairs of jeans and 1 borrowed pair of soft house pants; 1 tank top, 1 thermal shirt, 1 black turtleneck, 1 green sweater, 1 mustard button-up sweater, and 1 black oversized sweater that doubles as a blanket. I have 7 pairs of underwear, 1 "sleeping costume," and 5 pairs of socks (1 has penguins on it). I have 1 pair of winter snow boots (on 1 boot the zipper is broken), a winter coat, a hat, a scarf, and a pair of mittens.

The city of Mykolaiv[17] has compiled a list of 40 items its defenders (Armed Forces of Ukraine, National Police, local police, Territorial Defense units, Regional Guards, etc.) need, including: 1000 bulletproof vests, 10 reconnaissance quadcopters, 300 Motorola DR4400 walkie-talkies, 1000 head-lamps/flashlights, 500 sleeping bags, 10 minibuses, 50 axes, 20 chainsaws, 20 generators, 200 shovels, 500 power banks, 500 staple guns, 10 boxes of masking/packing tape, 2000 pairs of underwear, 5000 pairs of socks.

P.S. If you want to help source/buy/donate/ship any of these things for our defenders, please contact me personally.

---

17   I met Oleksandr Tereshchenko, a decorated Ukrainian veteran and staunch advocate for disabled vets, through a friend of a friend in Lviv. That's how I began raising money for defenders in his hometown of Mykolaiv, a southern Ukrainian port city.

March 19, 2022, Lviv

Time divorced from routine, with natural cycles disrupted, is end-less. There is no time in wartime. You are entirely involved in what you're doing, and suddenly an hour has passed, and then the day. At night it is quiet, until the air raid alarm goes off. And you can never know, plan, or predict when. You have no "time to yourself," because it is occupied by the enemy.

The war burst into our life in late February, destroying rou-tines, neighborly relationships, social community bonds, buildings, bridges, schools, and cities. But by virtue of being here you join it and begin to live with it. It wears you down and you rest and re-cover and now the war remains a constant while life begins to reas-sert itself in these new conditions.

***

A week ago I cried for the first time. It was after listening to a Syrian playwright[18] on Zoom; we were both participants in a public talk about Ukraine. His presentation — and his presence — touched something deep, disturbing a fundamental sense of security in . . . my own solidity. I cried in admission that the war in Syria was al-ways just a fact to me, some information that did not touch me. And now it's my country being torn apart by Russian arms and air-strikes, raining down from the sky in deadly explosions.

I listened to the playwright from Syria speak coolly but not without compassion about how Syria was a training ground for Russia: they tested 300 new weapons there, rehearsed tactics for ter-rorizing the civilian population, and performed a massive experi-ment demonstrating the effects of instigating a "refugee crisis" in the Western world. Syria was the site of unspeakable atrocities while the world watched without seeing. I didn't see it. And I could not imagine this war in Ukraine coming next.

A wise friend once said (and she said it many times in those first years following Russia's invasion of Ukraine in 2014) that if

---

18   Mohammad Al Attar, playwright and essayist, Syria. We were both partici-pants in the Creative Time Teach-In on Ukraine, March 12, 2022.

you refuse to see the danger around you as you sit in your comfortable home, untouched, sooner or later it will come to you.

The Syrian playwright instantly shifted my perspective. Bent over the kitchen table in a borrowed apartment in Lviv, I cried for the Syria I did not feel, for the fact that its destruction is irreversible, and because now my country is being destroyed too. And I wondered whether our course will be the same. Or maybe something will be otherwise.

***

I've observed that our people, from the army and territorial defense units to refugees, are being supported by small networks of volunteers, what I like to call "bands." I have numerous friends working in different small-group initiatives like me, but we are working separately. And we are often doing similar things, like transporting medicine and humanitarian aid through our various networks, in parallel. Some voice in my head from some other life wants to interrupt and ask: isn't that inefficient? Well, no, it is working remarkably well. In these conditions that are constantly changing and unpredictable, you have to be alert and adaptable, quick to assess, think, and respond. And having a small group of trusted, familiar cohorts to think and act with allows for flexibility. Meanwhile none of these little bands can reach large numbers of people (the needs here are vast), but when there are many of us doing this work side-by-side—and not spending time negotiating or coordinating our actions with our neighbors—we are genuinely working together. We think and act for ourselves, but each of us is constantly monitoring the entire, changing, situation.

In the meantime I've observed other attempts—amongst cultural workers and in humanitarian aid or even crisis response—of large groups trying to address these large-scale problems. Is it that when people see a large problem they think it needs a single large solution, that the problem and solution must be commensurate? These large-scale endeavors put so much more energy into organization (procedure, paperwork, decision-making as process rather than act, this tragic heritage of "managerialism") and planning how to address the problem than actually engaging with it. Meanwhile people are trapped in cities under bombardment; defenders are fighting without proper protective gear; and people are dying from a lack of medications in this country.

The kind of "banding" described above is a way of acting and being that is particularly common in Ukraine, more so than other Western traditions of cooperation. It refuses to be retrained into some other mode, just as it refuses to be codified into a stable model. And in times of crisis it is Ukrainians' great power.

***

In the early 20-numbered days of February I was working on the English subtitles for a Ukrainian film so that the production team could apply for additional funding. It was a job with a tight deadline; I had intended to devote a few days from morning to night to doing only this. But I found myself preoccupied with other things: reading news analyses and prognoses; entertaining vague plans to relocate temporarily; taking my cat to the vet to prepare her for unspecified travel.

And then I was faced with the decision of what to prioritize: watching an hour-long speech by the president of the Russian Federation or devoting that hour to working on the Ukrainian film. At that moment, from the perspective of historical urgency and apprehension about my future well-being, I chose Putin.

Yesterday I asked a friend, "Did you listen to Putin's latest speech?"

"Not yet. Should I?"

"I don't know. I haven't listened to it either. Maybe it's not worth it."

Suddenly it occurred to me that now (in contrast to the last week of February) this war—even if we're defending ourselves from his army—is not about him, it's about us.

March 23, 2022, Poland

This feeling that I owe someone, everyone, something for being on their turf—attention, money, service—is a feeling I've known nearly all my life. It is the burden of the refugee, passed down through generations. For everything my grandparents were given—food, asylum, the chance to make a new life for themselves—I have to keep paying back.

I had to take back what they had lost and abandoned, entering it anew, stepping gingerly like one who is on somebody else's turf, to realize that I was taking on its form at the expense of my own. I had to go back to the beginning, to the root of the problem, to the motherland. It took nearly forty years to find the audacity to call something, anything, *my* thing, *my* place, *my* home.

And now here I am sitting in Poland. In the house of a dear friend and her mother. I want to be that version of myself that can be generous as a friend. But I am here because I need help. I need help taking care of my cat because I live in a country that is at war.

On the one hand I can no longer live in my apartment, in my dear piece of Kyiv next to the river, as I once did. On the other, I can't simply accept *not living there*. I can't accept the Russians making *there* unlivable.

The only way to stop being the one who is always deferring to somebody else's routines, customs, and propositions is to resist. And I need to do it from my own place. If someone tries to take that place or take it over, then I need to fight that fucker. While if I try to assert my power over another's place, I am that fucker.

As soon as I flee I become the ward of whatever.

I would have paid Marysia for the dance class. But she brushed it off with "Come on, are you kidding?" And at that moment I really was too tired to argue with her. Over that. But maybe I'm bowing again.

My confusion here is real.

Here in Poland people are doing so much to welcome Ukrainians. Maybe this is not the place to argue. Because here I am on their land.

As long as I am in Lviv, listening to air raid sirens going off constantly, I am in the right to refuse, decline, reject offers to leave my home for the comforts so generously proffered by friends abroad.

Please forgive me.

I cannot be the good, gracious refugee.

Nor do I have the mettle for combat.

I may have nothing but a talent for mobility.

April 1, 2022, Lviv

I am tired again. But it's a more familiar kind of tired. I want to watch a movie, to escape for two hours into a realm that's composed and self-contained.

Lviv, which was so beautiful when I arrived a month ago, is even more beautiful when dampened by spring rain. But the city now feels strange, ambiguous.

I want to go home.

My friends in Kyiv are doing important discursive work. One has written a philosophical text in Ukrainian.[19] Another is helping British journalists show the world how gruesome war with the Russians is. And one has written about the war in Syria, shedding light on its Soviet legacy. They're arguing with their European friends and colleagues, for what is at stake here is politics, the fate of politics globally, even if Ukraine and its political future are at the center.

Meanwhile I am acting as a liaison between Americans who want to help Ukraine and Ukrainians who have the capacity to do something with that aid. First it was just talking to people and listening, asking questions; curiosity is natural and leads with confidence when followed without misgiving. Now tentative networks are beginning to take shape, the kind that are based on repeated communication, action in concert, watching how you and the other respond to challenges in new situations, and what happens as a result.

Tourniquets for territorial defense forces in Kyiv; underwear, helmets, and funding for Mykolaiv's defenders; funds for fuel to deliver an aid shipment to Chernihiv; a promo video in English about the Ukrainian aid organization I volunteer with—these are some of the things that have happened.

I suspect that in these efforts—unapologetic reflection on Ukraine's heritage (past) and unflinching commitment to keeping Ukraine alive (now)—is the seed of contemporary Ukrainian culture.

But now I want to go to sleep.

Did I mention how good it feels to be back?

---

19   Later in the year I translated Mykhailo Ziatin's "Ukrainian Theorem" into English. See https://evergreenreview.com/read/ukrainian-theorem/.

Scene 2

April 2, 2022, brings the news that the Ukrainian military has cleared the entire Kyiv region of Russian forces, along with the revelation of what they did to the residents of the towns they had occupied. Names like Bucha, Irpin, Borodianka suddenly become synonymous with rampant rape, arbitrary killing of unarmed civilians, torture, and other war crimes.

The Armed Forces of Ukraine (AFU) are defending the southern city of Mariupol, where Russia continues to indiscriminately bomb civilian targets. Residents risk their lives to get out. Some make it to Lviv and share their stories.

My cat is now living in safety with my friends in Poland.

I return for the first time to my apartment in Kyiv. Half the city's population has left. Roads are blocked at regular intervals by sandbags and other elaborate constructions. Only vehicles with special permission are allowed to cross the bridges between the right and left banks of the city.

Kyiv is still under high alert and threatened by Russian air attacks, especially after Ukraine sinks the cruiser **Moskva** *(the flagship of Russia's Black Sea Fleet) on April 14.*

April 3, 2022, Lviv

There is a war going on in Ukraine. Complete with horrors that I can hardly wrap my head around, let alone stomach.

I see it. I hear it. I know it. But I don't feel it.

Bucha. This is where today's photos are from. The people are lying on the ground. We see their fingers curled permanently, hands tied. They are dead.

My grandparents told me that after the war was over the Soviets came to their DP camp to take back and repatriate "their" people. And our people, the Ukrainians, didn't want to go. Some of them committed suicide.

As a child I took this as fact: some people took their own lives so as not to go back "home" with the Soviets.

Later I began to wonder: What could be so awful that you'd rather die than find out? Could there really be something so horrible that you can't slip away, luck out, get by?

Today I sift through the photos and see: this has happened. Already.

While I've been trying to find $100,000 to buy a lot of bulletproof vests. Or tourniquets. Or underwear. While I've been carefully composing my sentences and emails and trying to find ways to direct your desire to help toward concrete tasks.

This has happened. In Bucha.

And it has happened before.

And now it has happened again.

Not only in Bucha.

Not feeling is a survival mechanism. Resilience is when you can see and you can feel and you can act and those things are related again. But the mind and the body do not see or feel or act to their full capacity—this keeps you from losing your mind or losing your life. Sometimes.

Maybe it's because I'm far from Bucha or because I'm numb from intergenerational trauma or because I'm protected by affluence (or even association with affluence) that I don't feel Bucha.

But my grandmother felt Bucha. That's why she didn't go "home" till 1975. That's why she made sure I'd be born in the US.

And in the first days of March she knew there was a problem.
She knew I had a problem. But I know that you, wherever you are,
have a problem too. This is *war*.

April 5, 2022, Lviv

I woke up with a song in my head: the 1980s Europop gem that we would warm up to in our Lindy Hop aerials class. "One two three four five six seven eight" typed into Youtube search and bingo! As it played at full volume on my phone in the kitchen, I almost cried.

Yesterday I met Anya, who recently arrived in Lviv after a harrowing escape from Mariupol. Some of her words and images are stuck in my memory.

"You're all crying over Bucha now. I'm not crying over Bucha. I've seen much worse. If or when, no, *when* Mariupol is Ukrainian again, you will see things that you will be crying over for days."

She spoke of the night in late March when the Russians shelled her neighborhood non-stop. When she emerged from the bomb shelter in the morning, the buildings, the hospital where she worked, were flattened.

She had kept working, looting nearby pharmacies for water and medicine when supplies ran out. These things had kept her patients alive.

That morning she and her friends got into a car and drove, dodging mines and shelling, to leave. When they fell under fire from Grad (Russian for "hail") rockets, they leapt out of the car and fell flat on the ground, covering their heads. This is what you do if you're under fire without protective cover. People from Donbas[20] (after eight years of constant shelling) know this.

It's something I've never done before. But I am a dancer. I know what it feels like to go from standing to lying on the ground. I've studied countless ways of going from vertical to horizontal over the years. I imagine this action while simultaneously feeling the absence of this particular experience in my body.

Anya knows this movement pattern. She knows the sensation of uninterrupted bombing. She said, stone-faced, "There are many things I am not telling you." We were sitting in the basement of a well-endowed university in Lviv, outfitted with a modern lecture

---

20   "Donbas" is a term that comes from shortening "Donets coal basin" and commonly refers to the area of Ukraine's Donetsk and Luhansk regions.

hall and ample tables and chairs for studying while waiting out the air raid alarm.

Every time there is an air raid siren in Lviv, most people go to the bomb shelter out of respect for the rules. It's a civic agreement that has no connection to the visceral instinct to protect your body from imminent destruction.

Anya says, "We know now how to tell by the sound of fire whether it's far away, close but not a threat, really close by, or right overhead." When they realized it was not that close they got back in the car and kept driving.

She told us the city had been investing in its roads lately. "Why did we put all this money into our roads instead of defensive weapons? Here I am looking at this disgusting Russian soldier with dirty pants and a bulky Soviet belt, this scum, standing on a nice, newly paved road. What am I supposed to do with this? Throw chunks of asphalt at him? Or into the sky at the bombers?"

"I don't have the vocabulary to describe what they are—not who, but *what*."

April 10, 2022, Kyiv

Now I am in Kyiv. The city is spacious, in part because of the terrain, and to a large extent because so many people have left.

Yesterday I walked along the Dnipro, in solitude, its cloud-strewn waters beside me. I feel strength and power being on my own land.

There is a substantial checkpoint at the corner of the street. The people in my neighborhood have always been serious about defending their territory: from speculative building projects, from suspicious elements in 2014, from Russian invasion.

Coming back brought the immediate and visceral sensation that while I was, really, at home again, surrounded by familiar things and landscape and daylight, I could never return to *that home* I left the day that missiles exploded within hearing range.

Even before recent Russian statements calling for the complete obliteration of Ukraine in the name of "de-Nazification,"[21] before the discovery of Russians' brutal murders of civilians in the towns surrounding Kyiv, I called this war a genocide. It began the moment that Russia's massive assault on February 24 sent Ukrainian people fleeing to different parts of the country (and millions across the border), splitting families, scattering communities, wrenching people from their homes and cities.

A human being is not contained in its skin; we need our places and our people to feel like ourselves.

***

There is nothing like sleeping in your own bed. The way the body relaxes. Even when it fears that it shouldn't.

There were no air raid sirens last night.

---

21   On April 3, 2022, Russian media outlet *RIA Novosti [News]* published the article "What Russia Should Do With Ukraine" by Timofey Sergeytsev, outlining a policy to eliminate the Ukrainian people, along with their distinct language, history, and culture—calling it "de-Nazification." The text justifies and encourages the atrocities and genocidal actions of Russian forces in Ukraine.

In Lviv I tried all sorts of responses to the sirens. Settling down in the corridor with my computer was standard. Staying in bed felt defiant. Once I slept in the bathtub.

One anxious morning I woke just after falling asleep, dressed, and went down to the nearby bomb shelter. Sitting there, butt freezing on the cold pressboard bench and inhaling the dank air, I felt stupid. The risk of injury or death from an airstrike in Lviv is negligible, but you are sure to damage your health from interrupted sleep and spending an hour in the cold, which creeps through the soles of your winter boots. Minutes after returning to my apartment I am already sneezing.

Being safe is not a state, but an event. As long as it keeps recurring you can restore your energy and wits to prepare for the next time you have to think and act quickly. Why fill these moments with projections of what could happen based on memories of past suffering?

One night in Lviv I had the distinct sensation that I was back in childhood, lying in bed in the American suburbs. I would often imagine an impending break-in or fire or some other disaster I had seen on the TV show *Rescue 911*. Only now—when my body is primed from its own experience of air raid sirens and the threat of bombing from the sky—do I know what that feeling of danger actually was.

I've been escaping from the Russians since 1943.

***

When you run away you preserve the memory of your home unscathed, even if it's decades before you return (or never). My grandmother took her entire experience of home, sealed hermetically by the abruptness and violence of her departure at the hands of Nazi soldiers, to Germany, then to England, and then to the US.

Decades later I received a love for her homeland and its warm culture of community as well as an obsession with safety. I also inherited resourcefulness, flexibility, and a talent for getting by in new situations. Perhaps I could have been a spy were I not completely occupied with repairing this severed connection between home and security (which has taken generations).

That rupture has made us, like so many millions who went through that war, susceptible to idealizing abstractions like homeland, safety, or peace. And the devotion to these abstractions is detrimental to life, to a life lived vibrantly (in partnership with death, which will come sooner or later anyway), and to political life based on freedom.

The first morning I awoke in Kyiv after my return, I sensed a process happening inside my body that was set in action before I was born. As if my primary purpose was to experience that incredibly uncomfortable feeling of going on living in your home, now in the midst of war, knowing that you are under attack and always in potential danger.

I agree wholly with my grandmother that war is something nobody should ever have to experience. But she misjudged in trying to protect me totally. Because what I'm learning now I'm learning for all the generations of my family since World War II: peace, like safety, exists in moments. Like when it's dark and quiet at night in Kyiv.

But I feel safety in mobility (thanks to my refugee heritage). And perhaps in nothing else.

April 15, 2022, Kyiv

Fear for my own safety is attached to my sense of connection to other people. Like it's my responsibility to them to remain unharmed.

Alone in my apartment, listening to the wind, I am not afraid. I remember that being open is something I can do, shifting the state of my body, relaxing to listen and take in and meet whatever is around me. The wind blows in gusts, shaking the metal casing of the balcony. It sounds different in the overall silence of the city. There is no human activity to absorb and dampen its power.

***

Spring sunshine in Kyiv and people are walking around outside, even during the air raid alarm — warm, radiant, defiant.

Back in February, as Russian troops were massing at Ukraine's borders and international correspondents were amassing in Kyiv, my friends and I were sitting in the kitchen and talking about how Ukrainians — now in the spotlight — have to speak. And show the world who we are.

To say Ukraine is defying Russia no longer makes sense. For that stands on an assumption, the Russian assumption, that Ukraine somehow belongs to it. But if we think back just a few months, the West also seemed ready to help Ukraine ease into a kind of submission that would restore the supposed global security order. Ukraine defied Western expectations too.

The choice between subjugation to Russia or obedience to the West was never a particularly palatable one. And so Ukraine just plodded along ambiguously, neither here nor there, but "not dead yet."[22]

Under increasing pressure and finding no safe path or protection, Ukraine began to fight. Ukrainians have been fighting valiantly and together, with the army doing its job and the citizenry doing anything to support them (from reporting on the positions of

---

22   "Ukraine has not yet died, nor her glory, nor her freedom" is the first line of the Ukrainian national anthem.

enemy troops; to taking down road signs; to feeding, outfitting, and supplying our defenders).
Ukraine has shown itself to be daring, tireless, and staunch.

**

Ukraine doesn't have philosophy. Ukrainians of the intellectual and cultural class tend toward abstraction and imitation, as if it were enough to utter the right words and phrases, to study European languages, and to maintain strategic personal connections. While other Ukrainians are so bound to their homes and communities that they don't know how to survive – let alone think – independently.

But Ukrainians have the audacity to do things. Without asking. Without thinking too far ahead. Without mapping out in their imaginations how it will work or endure in the long run. This great energy to do something fully in the moment is a basis for glory.

I remember preparing for an evening performance with my Ukrainian dance colleagues in 2008: one starts cutting the sheets of paper we were to hand out as programs in half with scissors. By hand. "You can't do that!" I cry out. The offices where I had always worked had precision paper cutters, or at least you take a ruler to measure and draw a straight line. "Why not?" she replies, and keeps on cutting.

The Ukrainians I consort with today, whether those artists in Kyiv or the volunteers in Lviv or the veterans from Mykolaiv, regularly defy the limits of my imagination. We argue, get emotional, and sometimes I walk away in sheer exasperation. Then I come back. Because there is something fascinating in that drive, in the way that their intelligence operates – not in the way I expect it to, but in some other way that forces me to reconsider how I understand intelligence, seriousness, commitment.

I can only imagine what the US State Department or Department of Defense has been through over these past months. I'm sure they would have preferred Ukraine's demure self-amputation of chunks of its territory through a process of negotiation.

Instead we too (everywhere) must quickly adopt this sense of exigency that keeps returning you to the present moment, where the nearness of death makes you appreciate being alive, which a person who has lived only in "peace" could never know.

*****

If Ukraine has "spoken" through action, it is still important not to confuse action and activity. The latter is the coordinated movement of a swarm of ants (with delicate communication, each member doing its part for the good of the group). Activity feels good—the movement, the cooperation, the sense of purpose that is bound to specific tasks, goals, and challenges (that can be met, accomplished, and appraised).

I've also witnessed Ukrainian moments of glory fall. This is characteristic of our recent history.

We can't wait until the war is won to discover and cement the foundations that support this constant movement. What does Ukrainian glory stand on? National identity? Our land? Our language? Our people, who are finally learning to imagine themselves as something more than their ethnic origins? Identity is now determined in action.

The need to fortify something from below is different from "Close the sky!" or "Gimme shelter" or even building institutional structures that will continue to stand when the activists get tired.

This is about ground.

It is already there.

But we need to see it and feel it supporting our weight as we stand.

We need to examine it, to dig in, and to know whose bodies were buried in it.

We need to know what grows in it and what does not.

We need to say what we've done on this ground.

These things matter.

April 21, 2022, Lviv

A week ago I filled an old hiking backpack with an assortment of things I might need in the next several months and said good-bye to my apartment with full uncertainty about when I will next return. "Never" did not cross my mind.

Tonight in Lviv the air is chilly but with the texture of spring. I have to make a certain effort to keep sensing the war when it's happening somewhere further away. Still my legs tingle as I think of the thousand or so people in Mariupol who remain underground in the tunnels of the Azovstal plant, which Putin has ordered to seal off, as if to exterminate those inside.

***

Yesterday while writing a letter to people outside Ukraine about what is going on in Mariupol, I nearly wrote the word "unimaginable" and then—stop, this *has* happened. It cannot be outside the realm of imagination. It is real; it is history, if you will.

I have spoken to women who escaped from Mariupol, taking in and communicating with them not only through words but also through attention, our bodies in proximity. I knew in the moment and know still that I cannot imagine what each of them went through. Imagination—its landscape and its limits—is always an individual matter.

There is a difference between "I cannot imagine" and "unimaginable." Russia's unjustified invasion and ongoing brutal assault of Ukraine, with its barbaric genocidal attack on civilians and soldiers outside existing international conventions of war, has drastically moved the threshold for what can be called "unimaginable."

***

I heard a story (from the person who listened to the person who experienced it): in Bucha the Russian soldiers (young and scared) burst into a bomb shelter filled with women and children. They had them stand up and then shot every other one.

Genocide is about destroying the group, so its individual victims are arbitrary. When you are standing next to someone who is
being shot the difference between you and someone else is negligible.

I'm a grandchild of World War II; my mother is a Holodomor
researcher; I've read Primo Levi. The cruelty that human beings can
inflict on one another does not surprise me.

The horror of what we have learned about what the Russians
did to civilians in Bucha and throughout the Kyiv region took time
to sink in, to pass through generations-formed layers of resistance:
from refusing to look (I have more important things to do, and only
after all my efforts produce no result, the photos from Bucha are
still there...), to sleeping on it, to disbelief—not that *it* happened,
but that I *am here* looking at these photos, that this is happening *here*
where I am.

***

There are two ways to lose touch with the war: one is by feeling safe
and comfortable and unperturbed (secure in what you know),
while the other is by entertaining threats and potential dangers (including that of nuclear attack) so that your senses become garbled
and clouded by fear.

You need to do something to make the events of war more
concrete—whether it's going to the place where it happened, talking to a person who lived through it, formulating a question and
looking for the answer, taking a walk or a shower, and remember-
ing where *you* are and what you are doing.

I've made a practice of repeating: I have never stood next to
someone who is being shot.

Not: How lucky I am not to be the person who was shot. Or:
How fortunate and privileged I am never to have had the experience of standing next to someone who is being shot.

Just the facts made proximal through sentence construction: I
have never stood next to someone who is being shot.

Such experiences form people for generations. My grandparents saw their friends—murdered—lying by the side of the road as

they fled Ukraine in 1943. They had planned to escape together in the middle of the night, but my grandfather had an intuition that it was better to wait until morning. While the friends left according to plan. How do you live with that?

What about the boy who witnessed his mother being raped for several hours and then she died? His hair went gray overnight.

Someone is already thinking about how he will recover.

I am still stuck on: How can I live with this?

***

I first felt shame on February 24, as I was running away from Kyiv in fear of the Russian advance. I felt ashamed before my sister in the US, who was absolutely right when she urged me to leave the previous Sunday, and before my grandmother, who turned 95 that day. For all she had done to plant me in America with the promise of a good life, here I was participating in history's repeat performance.

The shame of being a refugee — of lacking the courage to stay and fight, of failing to defend one's home and people — is the shame of leaving what's yours for the sake of self-preservation. It's recognizing in yourself the compulsion toward moving constantly, whether away from the site of danger or wound up in unceasing activity, so as to keep from feeling the pain and horror and responsibility of witnessing and living with crimes we are now learning to imagine.

Scene 3

As the reality of the atrocities committed by Russian soldiers sinks in, the number of civilians and soldiers killed continues to grow. You can practically smell the overabundance of unnatural death in the air – even walking along Lviv's quiet cobblestone streets.

The soldiers in the Azovstal plant in Mariupol produce videos to show the world the scale of Russia's attack, which has decimated the city while they continue to resist.

A casual remark made to family and Facebook friends on my birthday generates several thousand dollars to buy reconnaissance drones for the AFU in Mykolaiv. Now I have friends in this southern river port not far from Odesa.

May 9 – Soviet Victory Day, commemorating the glorious defeat of Nazi Germany – arrives with anxiety over how Russia might celebrate this year.

That day US president Joseph Biden signs the Ukraine Democracy Defense Lend-Lease Act of 2022. It's a powerful declaration of US support for Ukraine, eliciting parallels between the defeat of Nazi Germany in 1945 and an intent to defeat Putin's Russia (although in practice it's of little consequence).

The US and other Western nations are slow to see the fundamental conflict between Russia's defiance of international agreements through its unprovoked, criminal war in Ukraine and its continued participation in global partnerships, from the United Nations Security Council to the G20.

April 29, 2022, Lviv

My position on Russia is clear: Russia is the enemy. Russian soldiers waging war on Ukraine's territory must be destroyed, and any Russians who claim that Ukrainians today are somehow fighting for *their* freedom should fuck off.

Russia is waging a genocidal war against Ukraine. Russia has declared its intentions to destroy Ukraine as a nation and obliterate the Ukrainian people, their language, history, and culture. To leave no physical evidence to contradict its revised version of world history.

My grandparents taught me that Russia was bad. The Russian language was ugly, with its guttaral ы and harsh Г (pronounced "G" in Russian, as opposed to the soft "H" sound in Ukrainian). In the hyperpatriotic Ukrainian diaspora this was considered an objective fact.

But as I came of age in the multicultural US, where we were instilled with the value of tolerance, I began to wonder if my grandparents' ideas weren't of another time. Yes, it makes sense to fear and loathe the people who invaded your villages and killed your neighbors. But we were all living comfortably in the American suburbs, and when I went to college in New York City, I found that people with roots in Eastern Europe, like Russian Jews, were the folks I had most in common with.

It is not interesting, today, to say simply that my grandparents were right.

Instead I wonder about what was wrong with that promise of a multicultural global world that distracted its "citizens" with great international mobility and connectedness, while allowing for the rise of a country whose hunger for power and dominance could lead them to commit genocide in the name of squelching national spirit, or, in their words, "de-Nazification."

Today those Ukrainians who for years have been devoted to promoting dialogue, to transcending difference, to peace and harmony, are becoming more militant in their language and positions. I too am becoming more militant, not only against Russia but against anything that distracts from taking Ukraine's battle for

democratic statehood (and protection of its people from obliteration) seriously.

Now is the time to question universal humanist values, where
the individual life of the civilian woman who is raped and then shot
six times in the back with an automatic rifle is equivalent to the life
of the Russian soldier who killed her.

Because that is logically valid when you make political decisions based on economics (counting and calculating numbers) instead of on principles.

It is on my conscience that instead of interrogating the global
order, I demurred to it. As if that global order had already guaran-
teed me a place where I could be myself (whatever that means)
without fighting.

As the grandchild of people for whom blending in with their
surroundings meant survival, I learned not to stand out, to read
quickly and deftly what people expected of me, and to slide by un-
noticed. Instead of making demands based on where I come from
or what I stand for, I was busy avoiding danger.

It was only much later that I began to sense that I actually had
no idea who I am. And that that in itself is not good. You risk becoming a receptacle for evil.

John Demjanjuk[23] — the notorious Ukrainian-American auto
worker from Ohio who was tried and convicted in Israel of being
the sadistic Treblinka guard "Ivan the Terrible," only to be proved
innocent years later — represents the little-discussed darkness of the
post-WWII Ukrainian diaspora. He kept a vegetable garden and to
all appearances led a "normal" life in the US suburbs, while his past
remained on another continent, hidden from view. It was undoubt-
edly brutal, but we will never know exactly when and where he
stood on which side of the line between victim and perpetrator (I
suspect that he knew both positions intimately).

What makes him odious and tragic for all Ukrainians, to my
mind, is not what he did, for that we can never know with any cer-
tainty, but his evasive silence (which is decidedly unpolitical). His

---

23   See "Resisting the Temptations of Oblivion," p. 196 in this volume, for a more
     detailed account of the life and public trials of Demjanjuk and public trials.

silence was his stubborn plea to remain a victim whose fate is up to someone else to decide (whether his family, tirelessly claiming his innocence, or the court of Israel, and then Germany, using him to make a historical point). Had he said what he had done in 1943, he would be a man of action—even if evil action. Would that have reflected badly on the entire Ukrainian nation? Yes, we would have an anti-hero. But Germany has Hitler, and today it is a European power.

Demjanjuk's silence makes him pitiful and, by extension, all Ukrainians pitiful. How many tens of thousands of our people have had to die in the past two months so that we can finally prove our claim to our own land and that we have the spirit and courage to live as a free sovereign nation?

Today, April 29, 2022, is the first day that I asked: Why did I not demand in 2005 that Ukrainians in Ukraine speak Ukrainian? Instead I spent the next several years learning Russian to follow the most interesting conversations among local artists and thinkers. I liked the challenge and appreciated the stimulus since I was young and still open to learning new languages. But were I a bit sharper, I could have learned Russian to read philosophers Bibikhin, Mamardashvili, and Piatigorsky, and *still* demanded that Ukrainians in Ukraine speak Ukrainian.

They're speaking Ukrainian now. Only after the mass Russian invasion has made speaking Russian tantamount to speaking the enemy's language. For some people, it triggers their trauma. Others are ashamed.

What is wrong with all of us that only in the midst of Russia's genocide of Ukrainians do we begin to respond decisively to the fundamental questions of who we are and how we want to live? Why do we need the experience and evidence of crimes against humanity to ask ourselves what "humanity" is? Philosophy used to concern itself with questions like that.

May 6, 2022, Lviv

My fixer friend sends me a message: "Last night I was looking at corpses and thought—have I lost the capacity to feel? Where is my hatred of the Russians? But listening to the news this morning it came back. What right do these fuckers have to keep bombing my country? And I felt better, that I still feel it."

***

I never had any doubt that Ukraine must fight to defend itself, that this fight requires weapons, deadly weapons, offensive weapons. Every time I say "*Smert voroham* [Death to the enemies]!" I mean it. But I'm still surprised to what an extent the war has remained an abstraction to me.

Talking with military colleagues about what our units need (from different kinds of drones to transportable washing machine stations) and how much everything costs makes everything more concrete. I know how many lethal drones you can buy for the monthly salary of a Ukrainian servicemember.

I admitted to my friend Illia that the thought of joining the army myself is recurring more frequently. He said, "Come on! We've got three women among the new recruits in the volunteer battalion." My body that has hardly danced for three months is eager to move around outside: I imagine running and jumping and shooting things in the spring sunshine. "We're planning to send this unit into battle on Saturday."

All my further questions, driven by sincere and innocent curiosity, sink stupidly back into my mind. I admit to my friend that I am afraid to go into battle.

This is the closest I've ever felt to the war. Not because the person I'm talking to is preparing soldiers for deployment. But because I can imagine myself there, training. And I can feel the significance of leaving the training grounds to go into battle. And I can feel my own resistance to it. The only thing between me and battle is my own decision.

Which is a more powerful connection to the war than hearing explosions outside your window while you're going about your civilian business. In the latter case, it's an imposition, Russia's disruption of my life in Ukraine. Whereas joining a volunteer battalion, picking up arms, or fighting for Ukraine's liberty in any way — decisively and courageously — is acknowledging the situation as yours and that you are going to do something about it. First you. And only then are you together with everybody else who is also fighting.

Illia calls me the next day to make sure I understand that I am a greater asset to Ukraine's victory working at my computer, raising money for their battalion's needs from abroad, than as one more body in the line of fire. Yes, I understand.

That same day I meet a veteran medic from the US who has come to spend a month helping the Ukrainian cause. As we chat he begins to demonstrate the procedure for breaking open a door with a fellow soldier when you don't know who or what is on the other side. He guides us into position; we discuss where each of us is looking, how we start at different angles and then move close together to fill the gap when the door opens. It feels like a dance, this split awareness of where I am in relation to my partner and his line of fire, where my line of fire is in relation to my partner. Our focus in the exercise was completely on how we move together to never end up in one another's line of fire. But what about the person on the other side ready to shoot us?

I never thought my dance training might be useful preparation for clearing buildings of enemy personnel.

Until February 24, I was studying and teaching the Feldenkrais Method in classes, where students are encouraged to sense themselves moving through space, to become more aware of their timing, the subtle differentiations between faster and slower. Breathing. Reducing tension. In the weeks following Russia's escalation it seemed like this training would lead me to help refugees and people who had experienced traumatic events, who needed attention and comfort.

Instead, trained to listen to what I am really doing, to sense what I need, to clear space around physical sensations and emotions to be able to think coolly under stress, I've discovered a warrior.

***

My friend Roma was killed near Kharkiv today. Earlier this week I had sent money for his territorial defense unit and we exchanged a couple warm words in Telegram. He was a vibrant member of our Kyiv Lindy Hop community, a photographer and dancer. Was.

Alone in my room I am crying and angry and so aware that I am not the only one crying. How many people right now are crying for Roma? And what about all the other Romas?

I have to admit that everything I had felt up until this moment was not what I feel now. Now that a person who is one of "my" people, in the very specific, tactile sense, a distinct living part of my social fabric, has been killed in the basic act of defending *our* country.

The war keeps coming closer and closer, encroaching from all sides. Can you feel it enough to keep it in focus without letting it carry you away?

May 13, 2022, Kyiv

I woke up thinking about my passport. Though not about how it would be a great liability if I were to fall into Russian hands. Now everyone knows it's enough to be a living being to invite their cruelty.

Here it was tied to my attitude toward the war, to the repeating question: what can I personally do for the war effort right now?

It is a privileged position. The patriotic love I feel for Ukraine that compels me to stay involved in the war is purely voluntary. It stands on the fact that I don't have to be here.

Even in war, I'm privileged. I'm far from the front. I'm working at my computer and in my phone. I'm sending letters. I'm collecting money. I've had a Paypal account for years longer than any of my Ukrainian colleagues.

***

One afternoon, years ago, I was talking to my grandmother at her kitchen table. I had already been living in Ukraine for quite some time. Again I was asking her to tell me about how the Nazis came to her western Ukrainian village to take the able-bodied young people to be forced laborers in Germany. I wanted to know *how* it happened.

Did they come to the school while the children were in class? Did they demand that each family contribute one young person? Did they "ask" for volunteers? I wanted the details of how she parted with her mother (whom she would not see again for thirty years).

It was the first time my grandmother mentioned that they were sure the Germans were going to win the war. It was 1943.

My grandmother was born in a house with a dirt floor. Her recollections of that life always focused on poverty. Even in 2005 and the years that followed she could never understand my decision to go *back* to living in Ukraine.

Suddenly — a thought. It was nothing she said, but a feeling: did my grandmother's mother, watching her bright, vivacious daughter leave with the soldiers, think this might be a chance at a better life?

Ultimately, it was.

And it's that privilege of being born and educated in the United States that I carry with me everywhere I go in Ukraine. It's also what makes me responsible for . . . maybe not all of Ukraine or every Ukrainian person, but certainly for my own awkward presence here and what I do with my privilege.

***

I remember practicing dips in early February with my dance teacher: when your partner stops and bends you backward over his knee in one continuous swoop. It happens quickly, it's a change of orientation, and viscerally it's scary. What is the natural response? To shy away, tense your muscles, protect yourself. What must the dancer do?

"Be big, Larissa," says my teacher, "so that I (your partner) know where you are at each and every moment."

It is counterintuitive, but it is fundamental for dancing together, for partnership, for politics.

My privilege allows me to run to the land of my citizenship to escape from the war. My stake in Ukraine's democracy on its own sovereign territory demands that I use my privilege toward that aim.

Tomorrow in Kyiv people from the Lindy Hop community, which for years was a space of great personal warmth and joy, are gathering to remember our friend Roma who was killed last week forcing the Russians out of the Kharkiv region.

I could join them. But I can't find that warmth in me, nor a desire to meet those people in whose company I once delighted. It has transformed into a different kind of energy: cold, glittering, knifelike.

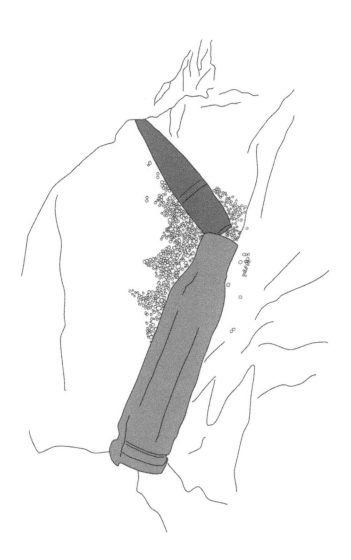

Act II

Scene 1

Mariupol, Ukraine's port on the Azov Sea, is now completely occupied by Russia, following the surrender of the remaining Ukrainian armed forces still resisting from their stronghold in the Azovstal plant.

In Mariupol, Kherson, and other areas of Ukraine that Russia has taken under control, residents are sent to filtration camps to determine their national loyalties. They face brutal interrogation to identify connections to members of Ukraine's defense forces, civic activists, journalists. Those with pro-Ukrainian positions face the prospect of torture, abduction, murder.

Ukrainian volunteers, aided by retired US military veterans, evacuate civilians from embattled cities in the east. The refugee collection points – with no military positions nearby – are regularly shelled by the Russians.

In the West, governments declare their support for Ukraine but limit the kinds of weapons they will supply so as "not to provoke Russia." Many individuals want to help – as long as the money does not support the fighting. Others say Ukrainians are too demanding: they should be thanking us!

I go to Mykolaiv, a city 20–30 kilometers from the front line, to join an AFU drone unit as a fundraiser. The city's water supply was cut off when a major water main was destroyed in battles to the east. Now saltwater runs from the tap, and drinking water is distributed by trucks stationed around the city.

Refugees from the neighboring Kherson region, currently occupied by the Russians, continue to arrive. Some people need help navigating their way through enemy checkpoints to safety. In Mykolaiv they need shelter, food, legal advice.

Everywhere you see evidence of Russia's daily artillery and missile strikes. The southern city, nestled between two rivers, is still beautiful in summer.

May 24, 2022, Mykolaiv/Lviv

I've noticed a direct correlation between the distance you are from the place where the missiles and shells are exploding and the scale of your anxiety about the potential threat to yourself or your loved ones. The imagination, wild and unbounded, fills in for the lack of sensory information. Whereas the closer you are to the source of danger, your senses keep you grounded (and safe). Up to a certain point.

I have never crossed the threshold to where your body is constantly in range of attack, where there is no respite from sensations of danger, where fear is visceral and completely justified.

My impressions of the people I met in Mykolaiv coalesce into a diagnosis of mass PTSD, only without the P. They are warm and quick, their laughter suspended above a raw, gaping wound of repeated death and loss.

Minutes after I meet Dima, he says a rocket hit the roof of his building last night and shows me photos of the exposed frame, remarking gleefully that the windows of his apartment by some miracle are still intact. The window of Olya's bedroom, on the other hand, is a sheet of pressboard, installed after a rocket exploded across the street. Her husband is in the army and was taken as a prisoner of war on April 12. Illia's friend Serhiy, a young bright soldier beloved in this community, was just killed — the day after receiving a vehicle bought with funds collected by volunteers.

It takes a day or two to adjust to the speed with which my colleagues move and make decisions in an environment that feels chaotic and uncertain. So many people, men and women, are in uniform. They take their AK-47s to strategic planning meetings, to lunch in a café, for a walk by the river.

When I can't sleep at night I read US commentary about the war in Ukraine and formulate arguments for why private donors should buy unmanned aerial vehicles for individual Ukrainian military units. We are using technology to protect what technology cannot replace: individuals with years of combat experience, skills learned and refined in actual battle, with an intimate knowledge of the local terrain and long-standing relationships with one another.

What these human bodies carry and can do is not reducible to data or a program. They are full of spirit. The way they work is unsystematic, infused with deep faith, and thus defies the kind of dull predictability that would make the enemy's work easier.

In Mykolaiv it was clear that now is not the time for grieving or even rest. There is a war to be won and one finds other (quicker) ways to refresh. I ward off waves of tiredness with vitamin B12, flat whites, and cigarettes, and make an effort to say kind, warm words to my friends who need a constant reminder that they are loved.

One evening I found myself in the kitchen of Illia's apartment, which was serving as a kind of soldiers' dormitory, including for two Americans. All the men seemed to get along merrily despite not knowing each other's languages. Kevin had asked me to find a local place to go dancing and didn't quite believe me when I said that place was Lviv or Kyiv—or the kitchen. But Illia was cooking, I had orders not to interfere, and Kevin put a song on the iPhone and grabbed me as a partner. The rhythm was unfamiliar but the general principles came back: relax, listen, and refrain from making abrupt, unpredictable movements. Laughter and playfulness and suddenly there was dancing in wartime Mykolaiv.

***

The body holds experience in neural pathways and patterns of tension formed to respond to the situations it has known. You can travel to another city, further from daily airstrikes, from the launch positions of the occupying Russian forces, but you are still wound up, alert and ready to fight, tuned to the environment that you came from.

When the body is invited to relax and move slowly you realize that there are layers of war between you today and the person who used to lie on the floor and listen to her sensations three months ago. And when a memory arises of stretching and sensing how your different parts are connected, as you used to spend an hour doing each night in your bedroom in Kyiv, you want to cry and you don't because it's not relevant to this moment and why are you thinking about this at all when your friends in Mykolaiv need hundreds of thousands of dollars and drones and organization and logical thinking to support a counteroffensive to win back large swathes of territory that rightfully belong to Ukraine?

One could interpret my restless movement around Ukraine, from city to city, apartment to apartment, as a kind of dance. Fact is, it's an old habit going way back to when I used to jet between the US and Ukraine several times a year. I came back to Lviv with the sense that my time here is up: I'm done running away.

Between the first time I returned to my apartment in Kyiv and my return from Mykolaiv something has irreversibly shifted. I'm through with being a refugee. It's time to stand and fight. There is no time for anything else.

June 3, 2022, Kyiv

Every return to Kyiv is euphoric. And each time — a greater intensity of emotions: elation, love, appreciation, horror, fear. Along with a growing resolve with which I say, I am here and here is in the midst of war and I am here in the midst of war.

An afternoon walk with my dear friend Larysa, following our usual route by the river, ends on a bench talking about how to arm and train the adult civilian population of Kyiv and surrounding towns. Because there are simply not enough soldiers in the Ukrainian military to protect us all from all directions.

Her friends from the Kyiv territorial defense are stationed in the Kharkiv region. They are digging in to hold their defensive positions, not advancing to clear the entire region of Russian forces. Because they have got neither the firepower nor the manpower.

Who is left to defend Kyiv? The seas of civilians who have returned in recent weeks to bask in being home in the spring magnificence? Right. Us. We are utterly vulnerable.

Walking home I'm thinking about how I'm not particularly eager to fire a weapon but it's something I should probably learn how to do, sooner rather than later. At least so that I can hold an automatic rifle with confidence, when scared, and be able to move deliberately. This is what it means to be home now.

***

It has taken me a few months to settle firmly on the position that the priority in aiding Ukraine is arming Ukraine. Now I have friends and colleagues in the Ukrainian military. I have a job raising money to equip a unit of the Special Operations Forces. Each week I meet another American who has come to aid in Ukraine's war effort.

Yet when I imagine a new Russian advance on any of the Ukrainian cities I could be in, I understand that all these beautiful, brave people who care about me will be called to immediate duty to meet the enemy head on. And I will have to do my part.

It is unethical to simply celebrate the heroism of Ukraine's defenders. Serving — your country, your country's principles (and by extension its future existence), your compatriots — is different from providing a service. And a large proportion of the Ukrainian people have been partners, supporting the defense not only through material aid but also with little (and big) acts of sabotage.

There is no amount of helping the military that buys you the luxury of sitting back and being protected. Our Western "friends" do not seem to fathom how serious this situation is or how great a role *they* play in stopping (or not stopping) Russia. We say that Ukraine is defending itself from Russia's advance and by extension protecting Europe and the West. But for all their crazy courage and heroic devotion the Ukrainians will not be able to hold off this monster with their wits alone.

Each of you, beginning with feeling–understanding–knowing that this war affects you, must do your part for this war to end. Otherwise it never will.

***

When I tell my parents over Zoom how I realized that I have to learn to fire an automatic weapon, not unlike the way they made me learn to drive a car at age 16 so I could survive in the suburbs, they hardly bat an eyelash. It's so easy, as a casual observer, to identify with a story you hear or a film that you watch or a thought that somebody else expresses when it's only in your mind.

In fact there's a whole process that happens when you are the main character, which involves gradual acknowledgment, questions, deliberation, and action. My first encounter with a bulletproof vest for personal use happened 24 hours after Lana, aware that I was traveling south, asked, "Do you have protective gear?" No, but I'm going to live and work in the city like a civilian. You don't walk around a city in a bulletproof vest "just in case." They're really fucking heavy.

It weighs 20 lbs (9 kg), which is bearable on my body, but lugging it home in my backpack it felt heavier than anything I had ever carried before. A 30- or 40-lb. child, soft, warm, and moving, feels lighter. There is something specific about the weight of a bullet-proof vest, perhaps in the density of the material, maybe in its purpose — literally hitting up against (and deflecting) death.

The next morning my body cried out in pain, "Stop changing cities so often!" With the realization that we are in this war for a long time, I slowed down and made some decisions, taking a long view and from a place of deep resolve.

***

It's easier to spend my war time in other cities and not have to deal with the psychic unease of living in your home with all your memories of how you lived before (in the smells, in the way the light falls, and in your movement patterns) and their dissonance with the present reality that you are at war, in war, that the war *is* your entire context.

On this 100th day of Russia's full-scale invasion of Ukraine I am in my own apartment in Kyiv in the midst of war and I am okay. Tomorrow I plan to take a full day off. See you on the other side.

June 12, 2022, Mykolaiv

Summer in southern Ukraine feels like a seaside resort: the soft evening air, water everywhere and those gray-green trees that the locals call "Southern olives." Instead of vacationing in Greece I've gone to work for Ukraine's war effort in a place where you can go swimming on your lunch break.

***

Within a day after arriving I am in an army frame of mind. You have to act quickly and decisively. When you fundamentally accept that your work and actions are risky, potentially deadly, you are immediately free from that distracting worry about where to position your body when there is an air raid siren. You hear explosions or the distant rumble of artillery, and as long as your physical sensations tell you the danger is not near, you keep working on whatever you're doing. You mobilize your mental and physical energy to complete specific assignments. Whichever is of greatest priority at the moment. Still, I hold the privileged position of not being in the army, so I decide what to prioritize myself.

***

One night Olya and I are on the balcony.

I say, "Oh, the quiet is delicious!"

A moment later—the low rumble, like thunder, of distant artillery. It's a pleasant sound.

My inner voice protests, "Larissa, how can you find the sound of artillery fire pleasant?!"

And Olya says, "Those are ours." Pleasant, indeed!

"How do you know?"

"Because we don't hear the shells land. If it were the Russians, we'd hear explosions."

Amazing how the body knows things more quickly than one's clunky intelligence.

***

The next evening I sat on the beach for an hour, watching the sun set over the water and listening to the artillery battle off to the left, trying to learn to discern by sound which volleys are ours directed at them and which are theirs coming in toward us.

June 22, 2022, Mykolaiv

War is a dirty affair. You don't need to shoot a gun or to have killed somebody with your own hands to be sullied by your participation in it.

It is thrilling (and a bit scary) to watch the anti-aircraft defense streak across the sky right over your head, two parallel flashes and you don't know what it is until their trails fizzle out midair and nothing falls and they slowly turn to puffy gray smoke and dissipate.

***

In the last hour before we reached Odesa, the startlingly bright 20-year-old who was driving me and the truck his family had bought with donated funds for the Ukrainian army, suddenly erupted. "You think this war is all about glory? That these guys fighting in the east are heroes? You have no idea. The things those men have told me when they're drunk . . . They feel entitled after what they've been through."

This young Ukrainian is training to be a drone pilot and raising $50,000 to buy one called the Punisher. We talked the whole way, mostly about Ukraine, a country that consists of its territory and its people, while its history jumps between sporadic past glories and the present moment. What if Ukrainians were to bear that history in its full, unflattering complexity, instead of avoiding its dark stains? Ukrainians stick together in constellations of kin and personal relations, and power is a matter of individual influence; "every citizen is equal before the law" is just a phrase in the Constitution.

Ukraine's victory is not some distant end after which we all live happily ever after.

After a fundraising meeting I got into an argument with a colleague over whether or not life in Ukraine would be different after the war. Would people continue to circumvent the law, distrust the government, and expect somebody else to solve their problems? He was convinced that nothing would change.

I said, "No, look at how people are stepping up as individuals to do what needs to be done, building new connections and ways of working together. If nothing were to change then all these tens of thousands of people killed, the cities razed to the ground, all this would be for naught."

He reached out his hand—shall we make a bet? "For one hundred dollars," he said.

I replied, "I'm staking my life."

***

I believe in Ukraine's victory. This is no practice of positive thinking. If Ukraine were not to win, how could I ever speak to those (Ukrainians, friends) that I failed and to those (foreigners, other Ukrainians) that I failed to convince? How could I go back to those quiet, unchanged suburbs in the US where life goes on "as usual" after having shed so many different layers of protection and knowing that others here have lost so much more?

***

War has different rules than civilian life. Still, it has rules (which Russia has repeatedly flouted). There is a difference between killing to save your life in the moment and murder. If you take the time to entertain the humanity of the one who is killing you, it will cost your life. When an entire nation invades your homeland, launching a massive war, each soldier is part of the body that is killing you. When he kills your neighbor, you know that it could just as well have been you—you just got lucky. Missiles are even more arbitrary and leave you no chance for a quicker reciprocal response as an individual.

The aim of Ukraine's armed forces, faced with protecting their land and people from a genocidal Russian invasion, is to destroy the enemy. Imagining all the ways to destroy the enemy is not civil dinner-table conversation. There is no other way to win this war.

***

There are countless people serving in the Ukrainian military doing tasks that do not suit or make use of those people's talents, skills, and inclinations. It is a huge bureaucracy that in some places takes its time as if there weren't a war on. It also has gaps and inconsistencies and individual people who use their power to realize things that they've decided, with their own minds and experience, will increase Ukraine's military success.

Being in a situation of utter duress (like when a fellow soldier is wounded on the battlefield or when Russia is still pounding your entire country with daily missile strikes for 119 days and counting) you must make your own decisions and act using your own wits because you have nobody else's at your disposal.

Your participation in the war means acknowledging your power to influence it. Your participation in this dirty business means taking responsibility in the moment for how you participate in it.

With growing intensity, while intermingling with the military and under constant Russian attack from the air, I want with my whole being to end this war.

Scene 2

Tension is rising as the summer progresses. The number and frequency of Russian missile strikes on Mykolaiv are increasing. Targets include a hotel, a business center, a university – all in the historic city center.

A two-hour drive away, Odesa provides periodic respite and train service to Kyiv and Lviv. Mykolaiv's train station was damaged by Russian shelling in April.

84% of Ukrainians reject any territorial concessions to Russia, according to a July survey.

On July 29, the Olenivka prison in the occupied part of the Donetsk region is destroyed by an explosion. Over 50 Ukrainian POWs are killed and close to 100 more are wounded. The majority had defended Mariupol from their base at Azovstal. Witness testimony and investigation evidence suggest that explosives were detonated inside the building, debunking the Russian claim that Ukraine struck the prison using a HIMARS (High Mobility Artillery Rocket System) supplied by the US.

The AFU unit that I'm aiding is moved to a new position outside the city. There's a sense that something is about to happen. Are the Russians going to advance on Mykolaiv again? Or do the AFU have something up their sleeve?

July 3, 2022, Mykolaiv / Lviv

It's a good morning when you wake up to the sound of your alarm clock.

Not like the other day, when I felt a light burst of air through the open window along with a sound: loud enough that, still practically asleep, I moved into the hall (between thick weight-bearing walls) and then wondered, I can probably go back to bed, right?

The next morning I am trained. I know the jarring sound and sensation that wakes me is not a threat to my life, so I stay in bed. I listen to the second one, the third, fourth . . . with curiosity. One of the explosions is not as low and deep as the others: does that mean it's from a different kind of rocket? After the sixth I'm dozing off again. Then the seventh. Now my body is alert; forget about going back to sleep. Eight. Nine. Ten. All this lasts half an hour. All before 7 AM.

2,800 cruise missiles, said Zelensky, sent by Russia into Ukraine. That was last week. 50+ were launched in one night and the next morning my friend said our anti-aircraft defense destroyed 30% of them. "30%," he said, "is fantastic!" In civilian life he was a commercial airline pilot. Now he flies drones for the Armed Forces of Ukraine.

My friend from the US says, "Things are really heating up in the south. Why don't you just stay in Lviv and wait it out?"

"Wait what out?" I reply. With indignation. As if an intensification in Russian cruise missile strikes on Mykolaiv were like a thunderstorm you just need to shelter from until the weather system moves on. As if I hadn't experienced nearby missile strikes the last time I was in Kyiv or back in the days when I was a refugee in Lviv.

"Wait what out?" is my astonishment at an insinuation that this war is some kind of conflict between two parties who just need some time to hash it out and then the air will cool and we can go back to... *what?* In this exchange she and I cannot possibly be talking about the same thing.

***

As I lie in bed listening to explosions it's clear there is still a lot of space between them and my body. Space for living as long as I am alive. This fundamental visceral understanding does not intersect with discourse based on risk assessment. Who cares if there is a greater statistical probability of me being struck by a missile in Mykolaiv than in Lviv? The only thing that matters is whether or not I am actually struck by a missile. Which could happen while you're shopping at the mall in Kremenchuk.[24]

I don't lose sleep calculating my chances of dying from an airstrike. No, it's you, my friends, wherever you are, that I worry about. I worry that by the time you start to sense the urgency of stopping Russia so many Ukrainian cities will be razed and so many Ukrainian people will be gone or maimed or psychically shattered.

It's obvious that Ukraine is facing an existential threat. Every day Russia is destroying the matter of Ukrainian life. Russia is bent on obliterating Ukraine as such. But have you not noticed that Russia — beginning with its covert invasion of Crimea in 2014 (if we stick to the context of Ukraine) — has been challenging and eroding the very agreements/conventions/institutions that Western international politics has relied on to support the existing global world order?

Do you not see the existential threat to that global world order and the values it stands on? Do you not care that those values actually be values and not mere words? Even if you think that order was flimsy and in need of rethinking, where are you in this picture?

You cannot be a bystander. How can I help you understand this?

***

Lviv is now a hot destination for Americans who want to understand better what is happening in Ukraine through their own experience. I can say as much for my friends.

---

24   On June 27, 2022, a Russian missile struck a crowded shopping mall in the central Ukrainian city of Kremenchuk, killing over 20 people and engulfing the mall in fire.

After a long and tiring trip from a city where half the population has left and half of those that remain are in fatigues, I meet my
American friends in a city that seems to have forgotten about the
war. There is a chasm between my unyielding sense of urgency and
their unspoken expectation that we communicate in a way and at a
pace carried over from peacetime.

It is only natural that we should be in different states, at different speeds. I remember going to Warsaw in March and struggling to tune to my dear old friend who had not had the visceral
experience of Russian attack. March was a time when the war in
Ukraine was still in a crisis phase, when any number of factors from
any direction could have influenced the development of the situation and people still imagined a swift end.

Ukraine withstood that period and is still fighting, four
months strong. Ukraine has won the respect of countries and people all over the world. Ukraine will not give in or cede its territory
or freedom. This is a war with two clear sides; it will be fought until
one wins.

And the fight takes energy, attention, resources. I don't have
the same reserves to share with every person who asks. I am now
well-practiced in triage. So it does not perturb me when my friends
are equally blunt about how much time and attention they can
spare me. What matters is a kind of congruence—of words and
deeds, presence and presence, principles and action. You can feel
who is on your side and we support one another; this too is energy
well spent.

***

I am okay. In fact, in the evening, after a run with my warfriend that
ends sitting on the beach watching the sky turn colors over the water, I am more than okay. I've found a person with whom I can relax. A person who challenges my patience, nerves, and mental
quickness when we need to work together. But with whom I'm
training and expanding my capacity for quickly identifying the
matter of importance and letting everything else go. Not in a rush
or rushing ahead. All in its own time and true to the moment.

Being alone in wartime is almost unnatural. Am I less afraid to die if there are others by my side? Is being amongst people— seeing and being seen—a way of asserting and sharing my being alive? I've found friends who place a greater value on the quality of life, on living intensely, than on the fact of life itself.

***

Still, I am disturbed by the sound of explosions. Especially when they come from the direction of the base where my friends are stationed. I am grateful for every moment that they are alive, that all their limbs are intact, for every time I get to hug each one.

Ukraine is doing its damnedest to win this war. But it cannot do it alone.

You can help. You can be slow. You can make mistakes. You can fumble. All these things are human and inevitable, even if they cost you the success of some part of your mission.

But you must stick with the mission. You cannot leave it to somebody else to do for you. When you say, "Not my problem!" then Evil steps in, smiles, and gets to work.

July 21, 2022, Kyiv

The past weeks have been full of activity. I recorded a video-address in English, sitting amid the ruins of a hotel in Mykolaiv, urging listeners to support Ukraine's military. I wrote an OpEd on why Ukraine keeps asking for military aid; it's still awaiting publication. I've been in Ukraine's west, south, center, always passing through Odesa. So many conversations with new people, trains, a seaside dacha, car rides, and chance encounters. All so rich with unrecorded details.

***

I am leaving my Kyiv home in a hurry again. This time I'm not running away. But yes, I am running. That seems to be the tempo right now. It's in conflict with my old mode — take your time, as much as you need, for deliberation, for just being stubbornly slow. The insistent slowness has been creeping back these past several days — along with other pieces of my life before. Watching Lindy Hop on YouTube; fantasizing about dancing with my favorite partner. Periods of a lack of a sense of urgency. But they don't last long.

Zhenya wrote: "Do you drive? There's a car in Kyiv that we need in Mykolaiv." Wink.

I don't drive standard. Or in Ukraine very often. But Maro does and he needs to leave tomorrow and a road trip sounds more fun than yet another overnight train to Odesa.

So I sift through my matters, letting the most important ones rise and the rest slip away. What have I learned at war? Decisiveness. Not rushing and yet not allowing your thinking to melt into an undifferentiable puddle of confusion. Sometimes external circumstances set the time limit. Sometimes your sensations say, "Enough!"

War doesn't wait for you to make up your mind.

July 26, 2022, Mykolaiv / Kyiv

I have talked to so many people over the past several months, people whom I never would have met in my former patterns and routines. These are my fellow Ukrainians. The ones who have stayed or come back.

Practically all the men (you know they are required by law to stay in Ukraine) evacuated their women and children abroad. All the women I work with have sent their children to safer parts of the country. In other words, nobody I know who is volunteering intensely to provide humanitarian aid or serving in the army is actively parenting at the same time. Even I evacuated my cat to Poland in March. Our attention is not divided. Ukraine matters most now.

Here are all these people who desire to live in their own homeland, working in cooperation. What is their culture like? Each one calls this land "mine," yet what "this land is mine" means for each is not the same. Nor does it have to be.

It is so interesting to talk to them and listen to how they think.

Again and again I hit upon a kind of impasse. A discursive impasse. A political impasse. Many of the men I talk to have the capacity to think quickly, broadly, and systematically to organize complex processes. Their intelligence sees problems and solutions. But people appear as abstract — functions or programs or a kind of dense mass that needs to be educated, persuaded, or organized.

There are plenty of intelligent Ukrainians capable of thinking strategically. They are especially effective at organizing processes that involve production, procurement, distribution. I've met men with a talent for assessing a chaotic situation — be it a Ukrainian business or the logistics of supplying a large volunteer battalion — and devising a system for making it work efficiently.

But then something gets in the way, whether messy reality or — more often — a person with power who just doesn't see things the same way. The person in power wants to go back to doing things as they were done and destroys all the progress that was made. The intelligent men say the problem is in those people who do not understand the benefit of a logical, streamlined system different from what they are used to.

Why do these bright people not look at their fellows as capable of developing their intelligence through tough experience, trial and error, personal reflection in a similar way to how they themselves learned? What if we were to direct a greater part of our intelligence to establishing ways of working that include and involve the people with power, in a way that could shift the ways that they work (via corruption, nepotism, connections, etc.) instead of merely demanding that they replace those ways?

This is also about Ukraine's armed forces, which are able to fight with ingenuity today because of know-how learned the hard way, repelling Russia since 2014. At the same time the army is plagued by an ocean of bureaucracy, a deep-seated culture of "fuck off" instead of actually doing anything, and bright active minds who know how everything should be done but don't have the patience to cooperate with the other elements of the machine — to see those elements as people with intelligence and the potential to grow.

***

Ukraine's Western critics (and friends) love to harp on the country's endemic corruption. It's true that Ukraine's social (and by extension political) culture thrives on personal networks and connections. This in and of itself is not corruption: it is the ground upon which corruption then flourishes.

But when someone comes along and says, "Your ways of doing things, the way you've always done them and the way that they actually work, are wrong," it begs the question: why should I abandon my culture?

The director of the organization I work for is a master of this classic Ukrainian culture of personal connections. I've never met anyone with so many, and who puts so much energy into cultivating each one. But I find this continuous investment in personal relationships (not to mention the intrigues and posturing and power games) draining.

Focusing on the personal cannot be the foundation for political life, for it diverts attention from the matter you have in common. Authority attached to a person rather than to their position has no limits and puts too much weight on the individual. When that person leaves or loses authority, what happens to the power to enact?

Ukraine needs the Rule of Law. Only the Rule of Law must be attractive in its own right — not just as a requirement for joining the European Union or as the golden opposite of corruption. What does it provide that is missing from person-to-person networks?

The Rule of Law holds space for cooperation in political life and offers a complex view. Instead of seeing only where you are in the hierarchy of personal connections (who has more power or the resources to do X), you see a world shared by many — equal and different. Demanding that each person act in accordance with the Law limits the power of those in authority and holds every citizen responsible for the common actions of the State.

My people in Mykolaiv are very intelligent, and their talents generally fall into two categories: maneuvering personal relationships or organizing group processes. Each of these modes of interaction falls short of being politics. While the latter involves people, connections, and acting together, what politics really stands on is individual speech — speaking your mind while addressing everyone, rather than one particular audience. However, present-day politics — not only in Ukraine — overvalues personal influence and the systematization of how people cooperate.

***

I arrive in Kyiv starved for philosophical conversation, something I miss tremendously in the war zone, where all intelligence and energy is directed toward decisive action. My friends here, artists and thinkers, and I fall into the philosophical mode almost naturally. But the next evening, when we get together, it's to learn the basics of tactical medicine and to practice applying tourniquets.

War life is not normal. You can feel delight, love, elation, but the driving force behind all your action is the need to respond to a constant barrage of evil. I feel simultaneously drained and activated. I hit regular lulls and lift myself out by force of will to do the next thing. I have brothers- and sisters-in-arms who are warm, vibrant, and intelligent, and we need each other. Though I wish to keep fondness and affection separate from work, I need their sweet words and hugs to keep going.

Sometimes I sense how completely alone I am. It stops short of frightening me; I know that I'm never abandoned. Still I miss moments of connecting with the universe.

Tonight from the balcony I looked at the stars. Even without glasses there are so many.

The quiet of a city under curfew is delicious. That quiet is something I will miss when the war is over.

August 6, 2022, Mykolaiv / Kyiv

Tuesday evening the courtyard, flanked by tall apartment build-ings, rings with children's voices. It's a typical summer sound-scape—except for when there is an air raid alarm. The kids are shouting and playing, when suddenly there's a loud Boom! Now the children are screaming. Boom! Boom! Boom! An adult voice faintly directs them indoors. I resist the urge to go to the window and look. Reason overpowers curiosity when you fear for your own safety.

***

The past few days I've taken to packing my backpack (computer, documents, etc.) and leaving it in the corridor overnight. Just in case. Just in case what? I just feel like I need to have my things packed and ready to go. Because I know that I've been late before.

We are all living with this heightened tension in the air. We don't talk about it. It is the atmosphere. It is the environment. You can't ignore the sounds. My body jerks, and I feel it but I don't really know how to respond anymore. One does get used to it. At night the explosions wake me every few hours. I acknowledge them (sometimes by getting up and going into the hall: once I'm there, why not go to the toilet or drink a glass of water?) and then go back to sleep. I lie in bed anticipating the sound and sensation. And when it doesn't come, I get suspicious. Is this the calm before the storm?

The sounds now fill me with dread rather than fear. When I know that so many missiles have exploded (16 here, 20 there; that night they sent over 30; four in close succession, about 10 minutes ago . . .) and I have not been hit, thoughts about probability arise. As the number of targets in the city decreases, my chances of being struck go up. And if it's not me, then it's somebody else.

***

Can you *live* in a place that is under constant fire? People seem to. They go to the supermarket and get water from the semi-trucks outfitted with a dozen or so spigots, stationed every few blocks. They go to the beach with their kids on the weekends.

What are children doing in Mykolaiv during the war? My friends, who evacuated their kids months ago, fume at those adults who did not do the same. Selfish parents, they say, sacrificing their children's well-being because they can't bear the pain of separation. It's not only a matter of putting their children in danger of permanent injury or death—the war damages their developing nervous systems and psyches for life and generations to come. My friends miss their own children tremendously, but they rarely talk about it.

***

I spend Wednesday at a "strategic session" aimed at clarifying the values, goals, and plans of a Mykolaiv-based hotline to help local people resolve issues caused by the war—from searching for missing relatives to filing paperwork with the armed forces to receiving humanitarian aid.

Over beer in the evening my friend says the Russians have amassed 30 battalions in the neighboring Kherson region. They may start advancing by the weekend. This has crossed my mind occasionally this past week as something I might have to deal with. Even if Ukraine's advance to liberate that territory from Russian occupation keeps going well, Mykolaiv is the target of Russia's vengeful missile strikes. "It would be good to leave tomorrow or Friday," he says.

People in wartime, while incredibly warm when together, let go very easily.

***

Now I know it's worth packing your bags in moments of relative quiet. Once you are actually in danger, it is too late. And I recognize the lull, when enough time has passed after the last missile strike and the next ones haven't come, as the time to gather all my belongings. It takes little more than an hour to clear three shelves and a couple of surfaces and put everything into two backpacks to carry and one to send tomorrow by mail.

These movements are cold and pragmatic. So different from how I used to pack for the US every year, when you imagine what you might need in the place you are going and try out various options. There is no time for projection and calculation, only assessment, thinking, and action. I don't want to be scrambling for my bare essentials and fleeing in a sea of people all trying to get out at the same time. Who cares if I go preemptively? I can always go back. I don't need to wait for the mass exodus.

Friday morning I, my two backpacks, borrowed bulletproof vest, and a large bottle of water are in a car bound for Kyiv. On the way I learn that Mykolaiv is shutting down that night for a long curfew until Monday morning. My friend calls in the afternoon to say how tense it feels in the city, how glad she is that I've left.

Timing is everything.

***

On Thursday the Telegram channel, which carries local news (mostly air raid announcements and reports of the daily damage from Russian shelling), posted photos of an unexploded missile lodged in the pavement of Mykolaiv's central avenue. Right across the street from the hotel my friend stayed at a few weeks ago. By evening all that remains is a patch of fresh asphalt on the road. As I wait to catch a bus home, I mark its distance from the bus stop: 20 steps.

***

Arriving in Kyiv brings instant lightness. Though I miss my friends — and Mykolaiv. At night I hear a dull thud — a distant explosion. Or maybe a phantom explosion. May all those Russian missiles turn around and explode right where they came from.

August 13, 2022, Kyiv

Things move too slowly in Kyiv. I move too slowly in Kyiv. It's not that I'm relaxed, things just take too long.

The other night I went out for drinks on the right bank. Getting back home by curfew would have meant cutting short the time I had with my friend, so I decided to spend the night at her apartment. Really, this was also to satisfy my need to keep moving from place to place. At 4 AM the air raid alarm woke me up, powerful and urgent in this neighborhood. After briefly entertaining the thought of getting up and moving away from the window, I just lay there listening to its insistent melody. How many times have I chatted with Ukrainians about how the air raid sirens sound in different cities?

Aside from that, I've had a week of full, uninterrupted sleep each night. I finished a book-editing project begun two years ago that was disrupted by Russia's full-scale invasion on February 24. I've spent an hour social dancing, seen some of my dearest friends, and bought a jean jacket.

It's a terrible feeling to be living in Ukraine and think—did I not do anything yesterday to help the Ukrainian armed forces?

The power of Ukraine's defense is in the close and mass cooperation between the armed forces and civilians. As the war grows more concentrated along the front (which stretches over 2,000 km), without the daily reminders of people in uniform, army vehicles speeding through the streets, barricades, checkpoints, freshly shattered buildings, and the unforgettable sounds of explosions, one needs to make a mental effort to maintain contact with the war's urgent demands.

Still (and we know this from the years following 2014), the separation between citizen and soldier drains energy from the Ukrainian defense. As more time passes and repeating the same generic actions of asking for money and general problem-solving and crisis management gets tiring, the challenge is this: Take stock of the general situation and your position in it and decide what you can do well that most needs doing—quickly.

***

I'm learning to discern the different qualities and meanings of the sensation "I don't want to."

1. Sometimes it's the body saying, "I'm tired and need to rest. I can't do *this* any longer." So you stop and take a break by changing activities. Rest could be lying on your back in the dark, but it could also be a run or a walk outside or engaging someone in conversation . . .

2. Sometimes it's the brain trying to economize. Nobody (physiologically speaking) wants to think more than necessary. We often prefer automatic tasks, even performing useless labors just to avoid the real work of thinking, decision, and action. But sometimes something must be acknowledged (you know this cuz you feel it) and it demands *your* response. In this case, "I don't want to" is the whispered temptation of Evil. Courage is the antidote.

3. Sometimes it's you saying, "This is not my thing. It's not satisfying. The effort required to overcome my own resistance is draining." Maybe now is not the time, maybe someone else should do it, maybe it's something that nobody should do. Making an effort to do it anyway is dishonest and possibly dangerous.

I left Mykolaiv because it was no longer clear what I was doing there. Space, time, a change of perspective help give a better view.

***

War has taught me that success matters. Not success in the sense of feeling good or making money or gaining recognition but: did your shot hit the target?

War is expensive. It takes tremendous amounts of resources — metal, explosives, human beings — and destroys them. The point is to disable the enemy's forces to prevent them from harming and destroying you.

It's primitive. But it is very concrete.

In order to hit your target you need to know:

1. what your target is;
2. where it is located (distance from you, is it moving, etc.);
3. what you are trying to hit it with;
4. how your instrument works (what it can do, what powers it, what conditions it needs);
5. how you will know whether or not you've hit your target.

Most of the people I was working with in the army were not previously trained to do whatever they must now do to incapacitate the enemy; it demands putting their entire selves into learning quickly and succeeding in their task. Immersed in this environment, I felt for the first time what a privilege it is to work in arts and culture.

I've observed a disturbing tendency among intellectuals, whose material (knowledge, discourse, thought) is immaterial, not to respect the concreteness of words and concepts, to forget that speaking is action. If my words have not hit the target — if they don't express what I want to say — then I need to recalibrate, try a different approach, take a rest and return fresh, ask for help, train, find different equipment, etc., until they do. If you treat your work of thinking and writing with the seriousness and urgency of a sniper or artillery team, it may be just as decisive in defeating Russia.

Scene 3

In early August, Amnesty International publishes a report criticizing the Ukrainian armed forces for putting civilians at risk while defending Ukrainian cities from Russian attack. It barely stops short of implying that the AFU is to blame for Russia's repeated targeting of civilians.

On Ukraine's Independence Day, Kyiv's central avenue hosts an unusual "military parade" – an exhibition of destroyed Russian tanks and equipment.

I travel to the US to visit family and old friends. This involves taking a train to Warsaw, as Ukraine's airspace is closed to civilian flights and its airports have been damaged by missile strikes. I visit my cat en route.

September brings news of Ukraine's surprise counteroffensive. In the first week, the AFU succeed in retaking 8,000 sq km. By the end of the month they've returned nearly the entire Kharkiv region to Ukrainian control.

Friends report that the mood in Ukraine is one of joy without bloodthirst.

Recovering cities like Izium from occupation reveals the evidence of more Russian war crimes. Mass graves are filled with the bodies of civilians. Some have signs of torture, tied hands, rope around the neck.

August 23, 2022, Poland

Every morning at 9 AM the Ukrainian Internet TV news stream holds a minute of silence. Marked out in solemn beats, it feels long. You can actually do a lot in that time. It is to remember all the Ukrainian soldiers and civilians who have died in the past six months of war: nearly 15,000, according to official figures. You understand the number is conservative.

It must be hard for someone who has always lived in the US — a country whose land has never been invaded by a foreign country and that maintains a professional army that engages in combat on other people's lands — to imagine the situation all Ukrainians find themselves in.

For the past half year everyone in Ukraine has been under constant attack. To say that artists, teachers, engineers, nurses, IT workers, businesspeople, performers, etc., have all made defending their homeland a priority makes it sound like they could have easily made a different choice. I know that many people outside Ukraine think capitulation, ceding territory, or convincing everyone on all sides to peacefully agree to put down their arms is possible. They are blind to what is actually going on in Ukraine.

***

When the phrase "Все буде Україна [Everything will be Ukraine]" first burst into the air in late February, I protested. Too grandiose and grabby. Aren't we fighting against the desire to take over the entire world? But as Ukrainian flags have appeared in points around the globe and the Ukrainian national anthem is played at Finnish landmarks popular with Russian tourists, this affirmation is coming to mean something different.

Patriotism is a feeling that binds you to your homeland, no matter where you are in relation to it. This love for your land, culture, people moves you to action. "Ukraine" is coming to represent the courage and will to stand up and fight for what is yours. To give your life to prevent your place in the world from being usurped or destroyed.

Ukraine's spirited fight to regain full control of all the land within its borders is an antidote to the Soviet Union, whose legacy festers within and without Ukraine to this day. Contemporary Ukraine arose from this boundless totalitarian project, where citizens were the property of the State and subject to a constant campaign of terror by the pervasive secret police (think of Russia today). Ukraine's current resistance is an act of limiting the undead USSR's expansion in space and in time.

Like the citizens' militias whose history travels from the ancient Greek city-states to the medieval Swiss Confederacy to the "well-regulated militia" that was the premise for Americans' constitutional right to bear arms, Ukraine's military defense is empowered by its closeness to the land (home), the people (citizen cooperation), and the virtue of defending what is yours.

Where have people today gotten the idea that coordinated military action and destruction of the enemy to protect yourself, your land, and your people is bad? Even more dangerous is the idea that we can protect ourselves by not even letting our thinking go in that direction. What is the ideological heritage of wishing to delegate the protection of what is one's own (land, interests, people) to somebody else, or expecting the state or army or "peace" to take care of it for you? And whose interests does the avoidance of thinking about and participating in military action serve?

***

You can understand so much about the Ukrainian army by looking at how they're dressed. Each person's uniform is cobbled together from such a variety of sources (brand-new gear bought by friends and family, Ukrainian-made and -issued uniforms, US army surplus, German T-shirts adorned with the German flag, etc.) that no two are exactly alike.

Until recently, I had imagined that the army, where commands and discipline and routine limit your freedom to do as you like, would stifle the individual or at least make one's uniqueness less distinct. Perhaps it is that way in long-standing, well-organized armies that have developed systems for turning their members into effective elements in a machine. In Ukraine's armed forces I discovered quite the opposite: when everyone is dressed more or less alike, individual differences — in face, manner, posture, movement, voice, temperament — are even more visible.

At the ceremony where new members swore an oath to serve Ukraine last June, I watched dozens of fresh soldiers step out to face the ranks of their brothers- and sisters-in-arms and, reading from a sheet of paper, vow to serve their country. Some read as quickly as possible before practically running back to their place in the ranks; others declaimed expressively, like they were used to addressing an audience, intoning their conviction. In each reading, while accepting the same exact duty to devote one's life to serving one's country, the speed and grace or awkwardness with which each person moved and spoke revealed so much about them.

I too wanted to say "I serve the Ukrainian state" out loud, witnessed by ranks of Ukrainian volunteer soldiers. Later the commander of the battalion told me that as an American volunteer I am not allowed to take this oath. I felt disappointment, but also relief.

In the army, no matter what the command or assignment, *you* are the one who is doing it (or not doing it). This too is how citizenship should work. In the constant urgency of war, which demands constant response, you ultimately have only your own wits, intelligence, experience, and spirit to rely on. You have power, limited resources, will, and desire. What you do with those things will change the course of the entire situation.

***

From casual conversations with journalists and members of the armed forces, I've learned that the Ukrainian army has been adopting principles used by NATO armies for coordinating action between individuals and between units in battle. For example, instead of giving commands, superiors express intentions. Units on the ground act according to general, coordinated goals, but have the autonomy to adjust their tactics to respond to the situation unfolding on the ground. This is radically different from the Soviet hierarchical military structure (which Russia follows to this day), where

commands are passed down a long chain. This makes our job easier, because you can disable an entire battalion by eliminating a
high-level commander. Whatever the Ukrainian armed forces are
doing and how, it must be working, based on their ongoing successes in battle.

I look toward the Ukrainian army with hope that the experiences of individual citizen-soldiers will lead to more general
changes in Ukrainian society. Still, as we witness the heroic deeds
performed by military service members, we cannot ignore how war
damages and changes people. Our servicemen and women are sacrificing something of themselves *now* so that we may all have a
country and a land to live in. Those of us without combat duties
must keep working in parallel to make our society and political
structure worthy of the citizenry who will win this war.

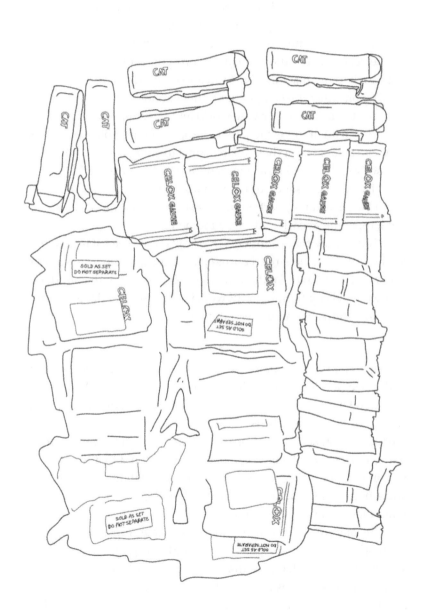

August 31, 2022, USA

At Newark Airport I ask a woman standing in front of a ticket machine if it's for the AirTrain. She doesn't respond. It's been a long journey, maybe I've forgotten how to put sentences together. I ask again. She turns and says, "I'm having a conversation." (I did not see her earbuds.) "I didn't hear a word you said," she adds, then goes back to the machine. No "I'm sorry, could you repeat it?" No aggression either. Just a light but nonnegotiable brush-off. Who are you to intrude into my private world and interrupt my private conversation with an invisible person happening in public space? The way you swat away a fly that's buzzing around you — it's annoying but not worthy of acknowledgment or even the effort to kill it.

The greatest shock upon arriving in the US is that there is a (tremendously large) part of the world where the war in Ukraine is not happening at each and every moment.

But I know that countless Americans have been standing tirelessly with Ukraine since February 24: I see and feel this support every day from afar. Without it we could not say with confidence that we will keep fighting until we win. To say that I deeply appreciate this support is an understatement.

***

Perhaps I had to travel all this way to see that people here cannot really imagine the war in Ukraine. How could they? And in fact they don't need to. Some people recognize the evil in Russia's invasion from what it awakens in their genetic memory. Some people see the unmistakable violation of a sovereign territory and the murder of innocent civilians. Some people understand that Russia's invasion of Ukraine is a threat to the very foundations of democracy and a free world. And if we wish to keep enjoying this world we've built, then we must defend it fiercely.

Reconstructing the war and its events at a distance requires great effort, and it's no wonder that people stop making it. That we should expect or demand that effort constantly from everyone, even from ourselves, is unnatural. It is unnatural to live in a mental construct or, in more prosaic terms, a fantasy world. Feeling bad out of "empathy" or "solidarity" with people whom you imagine suffering is not the same as caring. If all that happens is a change of mood, then you remain untouched by the war.

When your conscience says, "Pay attention!" and you cannot look away, even though it's scary, even though you are tired, even though you risk losing . . . something in you shifts—subtly and fundamentally. When you are moved to action (whether by conscience or by external circumstances), the experience changes you. This war is unnatural and to keep living as before means to normalize it and to let it last forever.

What I cannot get used to (no matter how long this goes on) is *each* missile strike, each university building, hotel, hospital, school, residence, etc., destroyed. Each and every person (soldier or civilian) killed in the war, who will *never again* delight us with their movement and warmth.

"Never again" is what the Soviets and the Germans began repeating after World War II. It seemed like an expression of the horror that people of the 20th century felt when faced with the crimes they were capable of committing. They constructed an image of the future with the promise "Never again."

Please pause for a moment. To ban events or actions preemptively is either fantasy or unethical. For you cannot know what a future situation may demand of you. You only have access to the past, which you can examine and learn from.

"Never again" marks the violent end of life, a break in continuity, a wound that requires healing, after which it will never be the same again. Shouldn't *that* "never again" be the point to which our thinking returns? Instead of directing our energy and attention to the fantasy world of the bright future where we will never again have to . . .

***

About halfway between Copenhagen and Newark, I put on my headphones and start to watch an Alfred Hitchcock film. Thirty seconds in—wow, such lush 1940s orchestral music—and suddenly the screen is too close, the sound too stifling, and when I take them off I'm still in an airplane, shut in a metal container with hundreds of strangers suspended somewhere above the Atlantic Ocean with no chance to get out for another four hours (or to smoke a cigarette).

> i am so angry i am sick to my stomach i am so full of hatred and disgust for every single person around me right next to me this makes me feel crazy i AM NOT HAPPY TO BE HERE. NOT ONE SINGLE BIT. i am trying all i can to choke down the stupid old thought i want to kill myself. because it's not like a plan or desire it's the state of the moment in the moment i feel like I CANNOT LIVE LIKE THIS that would be a more precise way to put it. i don't want to pray god help me please survive this

This kind of being enclosed "together" with other people when each is staring into his/her/their own screen, completely oblivious to what's going on around them (I was reading a monologue in Ukrainian out loud to myself and nobody even noticed). Following all these rules: go here, don't go there, show a card, something scans, something beeps. We are not performing actions. We are not even performing rituals. It is not clear *what* we are doing or who we are serving and because of that, it is *not ours*. But then whose is it? Is this kind of activity without agency not a channel for the movement of forces of evil?

I've asked friends how they cope with long-distance flights and many say they take medications to knock themselves out for the entire trip. What kind of situation is this where the only options to get through it are to distract yourself (films, sudoku), numb yourself (alcohol, sleep), or use drugs to completely knock yourself out? For what can you do with the violent feelings that arise if you actually allow yourself to sense what you've agreed to (and paid nearly $1,000 for)?

***

When I travel in Ukraine, especially nowadays (before the newly intensified war, Ukrainians too were starting to adopt habits of polite self-involvement), I always have companions. They're often people I'm meeting for the first time, whether volunteers or military or civilians, in a car or in a train. We share the journey; I learn something about what's going on in other parts of the country (or abroad); I discover how they think. I think people used to take an interest in one another like that; it was, shall we say, natural.

Strangely, that closeness of sharing a room in a train sleeping car for 12 hours with three other people, eating, sleeping, being in your presentable pajamas, feels so much more civilized than sitting elbow-to-elbow staring at your own screen, isolated by earphones and "respecting the other's personal space." Why did we choose this degradation that we call technological progress? Am I the only one who also craves common space, free space, space for movement?

Ukrainians today are demonstrating to the world what it is to take care of yourself. It is not: go to the gym to compensate for your lonely hours at work at the computer and then to the psychologist to talk through your inabilities to relate to other people and find satisfaction in activities and a way of life that are fundamentally unsatisfying. Why do we not care about and take care of our places, our environment, one another, ourselves? What are we so busy with? How did we come to voluntarily constrain our movement in—and interaction with—the world around us, enclosing ourselves in protected boxes, afraid, separate, and "secure"?

We prefer to isolate and not breathe on or touch one another because human beings are dirty, smelly, disgusting creatures. Our regard for one another is indecent. It is dangerous, risky, frightening to communicate what is actually on your mind; to voice a question that could reveal what you don't know; to call into question the words or actions of an authority or one in a position that you think requires deference; to call on a person or organization to take responsibility for what they claim as theirs.

Why do modern "civilized" people keep striving to maintain their institutional positions by toeing the party line and insisting on civility when there is nothing civil about genocide, invasion, or flouting the very rules that bear up behaviors of civility? Why should I restrain myself if those rules have been violated, endangering my very life and way of living? What is the moment where it becomes unethical to remain civil and practice restraint?

P.S. I made a gross error in my last post. When sharing the clearly conservative count of Ukrainians killed by Russian forces since February 24, I omitted the tens of thousands killed in Russia's siege of Mariupol. I remember statements made by the city's mayor last spring estimating 20,000+ killed by the invaders' daily bombardments and shelling. This does not include those people—many of them children—forcibly deported to Russia. Never again will those people enliven Mariupol, which was their home. We must remember them and keep fighting to end Russia's occupation of Ukraine.

September 7, 2022, Connecticut, USA

How does it feel to be back in the US? Kind of like being transported back in time and visiting my past. Only the people around me are still in their own present.

In Vermont I had the pleasure of meeting members of an ad-hoc community of Ukraine supporters who stand in Montpelier each Tuesday and Thursday to remind passersby about the ongoing war in Ukraine. Most had never known of each other's existence before February 24. Over the past half year it's become a regular gathering, a way to catch up with one another, kind of like how the Ukrainian diaspora of my youth used to come together at church every Sunday.

When we speak one-on-one, our conversations soon turn toward family history and the difficulties of growing up in a Ukrainian immigrant family in North America. The experience of being an outsider, of making enormous efforts to fit in and be accepted, has shaped us for generations.

It is natural for humans to tune to one another. We seek acceptance and blending as a means of security. There are many reasons why one may not want to speak of the ugly deeds one has witnessed, endured, committed, or even learned about through the accounts of others. Maintaining the social bond with whoever you need to help you survive and recover may require concealing your darkness.

Trauma moves you to do things in ways that are often inappropriate to the situation at hand or even unnatural. I've spent an awful lot of time moving from place to place, compelled by questions that I can't answer by staying put; escaping from uncomfortable situations (instead of facing them head-on); coming back to the familiar with a different perspective; fleeing imminent danger; and moving for the sake of familiarity, as if I could keep doing what I used to long after it has stopped being valid.

***

122 A KIND OF REFUGEE

Several years ago I identified as "bi-continental." This was the grand ambition (which my body consistently protested) of "owning" my duality as a US-born American citizen and a Ukrainian-rooted transplant to Ukraine. Practically speaking it meant traveling back and forth between my apartment in Kyiv and New York City/Connecticut/Vermont, spending a month here, some months there, and basically a few years living in the constant fog of jetlag. I was saved by the worldwide lockdown in response to the Covid-19 pandemic in March 2020, which forced me to stay put for nearly a year.

When the renowned philosopher and gender theorist Judith Butler[25] asks, "Can I have it both ways?" — meaning that she wishes to support Ukrainians in their war against Russian invasion (clearly the "right side" in this conflict) *and* to maintain an anti-war position (which means believing that all military operations, including Ukraine's to retake its territory occupied by Russia, are bad) — my answer is a resounding NO.

But where does this audacity to want it all come from? Both Judith Butler and I are formed by the late-20th-century American Dream, where what *you want to be* eclipses looking and discovering and accepting and honoring who *you are*.

***

Old habits die hard. I came back to the US for three weeks because I (thought I) could. Almost like an act of defiance: Look, Putin, you can't stop me from making a family visit to the US, from going to my friend's wedding I've been waiting for since 2020! And he didn't. Nothing did.

When I found a ticket on an airline I liked with a humane schedule at a reasonable price, I thought — this is a gift of fate! I barely managed to pack before leaving Kyiv (as I was scrambling to finish a translation that was more important) and was ready to abandon the whole trip had my cab driver not assured me he could

---

25 https://kontur.media/butler (Ukrainian/English), first published in French in *Philosophie Magazine* (April 9, 2022).

get me to the train station with 12 minutes to spare. I had, after all, taken three hours that afternoon to go to Andriyivskyi Uzviz to buy wedding presents (and support the Ukrainian local economy).

I carried these things in two backpacks—one in back and one in front—first by train to Warsaw and then by public transport to the airport and then by plane to New Jersey and then by public transport to my cousin's in Brooklyn. It was a self-loathing pilgrimage, every minute a stubborn effort to follow through on my commitments to all these Americans I had told I was coming. Would they have forgiven me if I bailed? Probably, but it's like I was having it out with the universe. Or running a marathon (which I would never actually do): take a deep breath, focus on the immediate accomplishable goal, then look toward the next one, just keep going, tiredness is just a state of mind . . . How American is that? With a splash of the Soviet Stakhanovite shock worker, driven by the urge to achieve a superhuman goal. As it turned out, once I arrived, I only had the stamina to attend one of the two-day wedding festivities, too wiped out by war and travel.

Let me be clear: I am absolutely responsible for making the decision to fly to the US right now and following through on it; and the utter exhaustion and inability to connect with people around me is mine. But the missiles exploding in Ukrainian cities are Russia's. The soldiers occupying Ukraine's territory are Russia's. The intent to destroy Ukraine and its people is Russia's.

***

To put it plainly: It is natural to be happy in the presence of people you love. I love my parents. I love my sister and brother-in-law. I love my grandmother. I love my dear old friends in the US. But my happiness is slight before the overwhelming urgency of Ukraine's battle to free its territory from Russia's invasion, to save our people, and to build and fortify our political nation. The war in my home is unnatural.

I came here to bring the war to you. So you can see and sense this body that's been there. So you needn't get on a plane, put yourself in danger, or trouble your conscience about straining Ukraine's fragile wartime economy. Many of you, like me—whose families came to the US seeking refuge from war-torn lands—already know somewhere deep down in your bones and psyche what it feels like to be attacked by bombs and shells and shooting soldiers.

This is the present I've brought you from Ukraine: an angry, exhausted, preoccupied me, who doesn't have time for the peace-time pleasures we once enjoyed together. My lack of compassion for your everyday troubles is the natural result of being in an un-natural situation. And you are in this unnatural situation too.

Maybe I should have come home missing a limb. Maybe this body of mine looks too normal to convey the pain and horror that has me screaming inside, "Look! This is really happening!"

I am not satisfied by your relief to see me here intact. We need HIMARS, ammunition, NATO military training, active NATO and US deterrence. We need your political concern and political spirit and political thinking. I would hate for war to become the last re-maining arena for political "discussion."

September 13, 2022, Connecticut, USA

To the Ukrainian diaspora and Ukraine supporters abroad, whatever your reasons or persuasion:

Please keep fighting, speaking publicly — and to each other! I've had the pleasure of talking to many of you over the past few weeks — some old friends, some new — and a recurring theme I've noticed is a sense of loneliness. Yes, I understand now what it feels like to be crying and rooting for Ukraine from afar, in a sea of Americans who aren't living this war minute by minute, who have other concerns at the top of their minds.

But guess what, that is what true solidarity feels like. It's not about latching on to somebody else's heroism or attaching yourself to the "good fight" because you know it's the "right side" in this historical moment. Solidarity happens when your commitment is personal and clear and you may be so busy doing whatever you can to help Ukraine that you hardly have time to check in with your friends or compatriots who are equally busy doing all that they are doing to help Ukraine. But you know that they are there. And the loneliness you feel as you face the world (and the enemy) from your individual position is the reality of leaving space between you and the other with whom you are in solidarity. We needn't stick together like a bundle of rods — that's *fascis*, the root of "fascism."

Know that your thoughts, words, and actions matter. Yes, Ukraine's brilliant successes in sending Russian forces scattering from the Kharkiv region are the result of a brilliantly planned military strategy executed perfectly by tens of thousands of courageous, dedicated soldiers. But this glory would not have come to pass were it not for everything that you — and we together — have been doing.

I'm getting on an airplane the day after tomorrow. Please wish me a soft landing on the other side of the ocean. Your hugs and attention and sweet gifts of time by the water and in the woods, dinners, dancing, listening, and sharing have kept me grounded and energized.

We will win this war!

Love and fortitude,

Larissa

September 27, 2022, Kyiv

Going to the US completely changed my sense of time. I brought the urgency of war with me and returned with a sense of continuity, stretching back to before February 24.

The night before flying to the US I watched President Zelensky's address in honor of Ukraine's Independence Day. Actually it was a short film — his speech from the center of Kyiv intercut with an impressionistic story of what Ukrainians have lived through over the past half year. I cried at minute 5, again at minute 6, and then when the sky exploded behind the young heroine who weaves through wreckage, suffering, and the courageous defense of our country.

Listening to the familiar sound of the air raid siren, watching a sea of cars slowly crawling westward, scenes from a crowded, darkened train station, anxious women and children huddled in a basement, the measured warmth and focus of ordinary citizens-become-armed-forces, I saw my own experiences of the past six months. This story of transformation, from uncertainty and fear for your life to accepting your duty and power to defend your home, is mine.

I grew up watching television and Hollywood movies. That's what kids did in the US suburbs in the late 20th century. I imagined myself in those scenes and then suffered from the constant disappointment that I was nothing like any of those TV characters. It was a culture of endless aspiration and perpetual falling short. Whatever I *was* did not seem relevant enough to really take an interest in, as if it was a private matter best kept to myself.

And now: the president of Ukraine is on TV telling my story. While millions of other Ukrainians can also say, "This is my story." How remarkable and strange. This is not a matter of identification, of seeing something outside you and thinking, "I want to be like that." It is recognition of something that has happened to us.

This is the difference between the culture of projection and anticipation that has taken firm hold of Western minds and discourse and the culture of action in real time that Ukraine is now demonstrating to the whole world as another possibility.

***

This is really happening is the lesson the war has taught me that I never want to forget. Now when I get a hint of a feeling, it must be addressed. You can't wish it away. How I longed to keep sleeping in the wee hours of the morning on February 24. *Was that sound really an explosion? I don't know what to do. Can't I just go back to sleep? Maybe it will pass?* No, that is what it means to be an adult—to accept that this is really happening. And what you do or don't do matters. And whatever it is, it's on your conscience.

Under the duress of war in Ukraine we don't make decisions from a place of leisurely deliberation: Who do I want to be? If I want to be like this, then what do I have to do to become it? The kind of reverse cause and effect logic, where you first imagine the desired result and then figure out how to get there, may make sense in developing procedures that demand coordinated action in which timing and sequence matter. But it has no place in politics.

When talking about ethical—and political—human beings (as opposed to human-like automatons or elements of a system) the fundamental question is "Who am I?" The answer is refined through action in one's environment: how you respond to a situation reveals something about who you are.

Perhaps this is why I was so disheartened by the ending of *Don't Look Up,*[26] watching those nice, reasonable, intelligent folks—the ones that most resembled me—talking about how they like their coffee and admitting that convenience store apple pie actually tastes alright as they await the end of the world. Do I want to spend the last moments of Earth's existence sitting around a table making chitchat?

Americans have lost a sense of finality and timeliness. And this impedes action.

***

My Ukrainian friends don't believe me when I say that Americans don't talk about politics in casual conversation. "What do they talk about then?" they ask in serious wonder. What we're going to eat

---

26   *Don't Look Up*, 2021, dir. Adam McKay.

or where. Whether you like this or that. Are you comfortable? How do you feel? What do you want to do?

I have one American friend who likes to debate. Every time I visit he brings up some controversial issue — let's discuss! I enjoy those discussions, but they almost always end in an impasse: one person citing sources to support their position, the other bringing up personal experience or other sources to argue their point. There is no common measure: the sources are different and they don't match up. You have to then argue about the legitimacy of each source, recheck the statistics and find out where they come from. Or it's your word against mine, but if we respect everyone's personal subjective experience, then who's to say mine is more valid than yours, or vice versa?

This is the ground that Russia is trying to play on when it makes outrageous claims that the bodies with tied hands and signs of torture discovered in Izium in mass graves after its occupying forces retreat are not evidence of war crimes committed by its soldiers but "faked" by Ukrainians to make Russia look bad.[27] When it comes to claiming that a vast majority of people on occupied Ukrainian territory voted to join Russia,[28] there is no attempt to feign legitimacy. This is a show of the deepest scorn for democratic institutions and citizens' participation in government.

***

---

27   In mid-September 2022, after the Ukrainian armed forces recaptured most of the Kharkiv region, investigators found several mass graves in the woods around Izium. One site contained at least 440 bodies, 414 of them civilians. "Most of the dead showed signs of violent death and 30 had marks of torture. There are bodies with ropes around their necks, bound hands, broken limbs, and gunshot wounds. Several men exhibited genital amputation," according to Kharkiv regional military administration head Oleh Synegubov (September 23; https://t.me/synegubov/4304).

28   On September 23–27, Russian occupation authorities staged referendums in parts of four regions of Ukraine under their temporary control. Electoral officials accompanied by armed soldiers went from house to house to collect votes. Leaders of the parts of the Donetsk and Luhansk regions occupied by Russia since 2014 claimed around 99% of their populations wanted to join Russia.

What is utterly disappointing in the two endings of *Don't Look Up* is the refusal of American culture to deal with danger. One group, let's call them the Left, seeks meek acceptance of its own demise in the creature comforts of food and family, while the other, which conjures the Right, dreams up a project to get rich, takes a risk, and then escapes to save itself. The world is doomed: *both* camps are ready to throw it all away rather than caring about and taking care of it.

As a young person in the US, I never believed that what I thought or did had any bearing on the structure, function, or actions of my country and its government (like launching the second Iraq War). I had no idea that the world is mine to take care of. And that if I don't, nobody else will do it for me. In fact I was convinced that the world was already taken care of, that my job was to find my place in it, and whether I did or not was merely a matter of my own personal un/happiness.

American culture does not encourage asking questions. Criticizing is okay. Voicing your opinions—oh god, yes. But asking questions is forward, impolite, nosy. Even if not perceived as a threat or as challenging the other's authority, it comes across as awkward, like something a sophisticated person would never do. Why didn't you Google it?

Leaving your home is a very serious act, something that should not be undertaken unless you absolutely must. What if my exodus to Ukraine at age 25 to the land my family had left behind was also a sort of cop-out? It was easier for me to move halfway round the world from the place I had grown up in to a place where I knew next to nobody and which I knew next to nothing about, than to ask questions of my parents and the greater Ukrainian diaspora community about that land and their lives before. It was far easier to abandon my fellow Americans than to ask them: Who are you and what are we doing here together?

Entr'acte

Ukrainian Is a Place I Want to Live

Regina takes the phone, utters a word in Russian, then stops — instantly realizing "Larissa is not one of my Russian-speaking family members" — and starts speaking Ukrainian. In that instant I'm flooded with love. Not because we've never spoken Ukrainian to one another, not because it's the first time I've admired this woman who is also fluent in French and English. It's the event itself: I'm talking to Regina — an Odesan who lives in Paris and is speaking to me from London — in Ukrainian. We don't talk for a long time, but the exchange feels warm, sincere, and intimate.

Is there something about the Ukrainian language that lends itself to this sort of communication? It would be too easy to romanticize. I think it's the decision — made by each of us, together — that Ukrainian will be the medium for what we have to say to one another.

After February 24, the decision to speak Ukrainian became a mass phenomenon. Russian, after all, is the language of the enemy.

***

In March I'm walking through the park in Lviv: a young mother with her toddler is making an effort to find the Ukrainian word for "swan." "Is it really so similar to the Russian лебедь?" her expression seems to say. Judging from her appearance, she's well-off and probably came from Kyiv or some city further east. Now, with nobody watching (as opposed to the way some politicians demonstratively speak the national language), she struggles to speak Ukrainian to her son. It's a personal existential matter. A short distance away, her well-dressed husband paces with his mobile phone, maintaining an animated conversation in Russian.

I had a dream, or maybe it was a fantasy, in springtime Lviv: I imagined an attractive, unfamiliar man who spoke Ukrainian with an accent.

"So what?" you may ask. "People speak English with an accent all the time." Until recently, people who spoke Ukrainian with an accent were incredibly rare.

Ukrainian speakers generally fall into one of two categories. Some grew up speaking Ukrainian at home, naturally. Others have made a point of learning and speaking it as conscientious Ukrainian citizens. Members of both groups take pride in speaking it properly, weeding out Russian words that may slip in through ignorance or habit, emphasizing the grammar and turns of phrase that are uniquely Ukrainian. With no academy devoted to preserving the purity of the Ukrainian language, it's up to individuals to promote and police the right way to speak it. My friends are always quick to point out when I make a grammatical mistake or use English syntax to organize my Ukrainian words.

When I first arrived in Ukraine, speaking my distinct diaspora dialect, the locals couldn't always understand me, especially in central Ukraine, further from big cities. It wasn't that these people had never heard Ukrainian, but I suspect they'd never heard someone who spoke it differently. Their ears weren't trained to be flexible enough to accept my unusual expressions, my intonation, and even the slowness with which I formulated thoughts. My friends were also impatient Soviet-raised Ukrainians who would try to finish my sentences, tell me what I'm thinking, or interject with "just say it in English" as if I were performing a translation in my mind as they struggled to wait for the words to come out.

Now it is I who listens patiently as my friend Artur struggles to find the right Ukrainian words. Before February 24, he had always spoken Russian eloquently and unabashedly, but this did not make him any less Ukrainian — he was from Dnipro. Our conversations manifested that classic Ukrainian phenomenon of one person speaking Russian and the other Ukrainian, and while both understand each other, each prefers to keep speaking their own language.

Today my Ukrainian friends Artur, Kostia, Dima, and Andriy are making a visible effort to speak Ukrainian. While foreigners like Kevin, Bill, and Marcel, whom I've met this year, are so drawn to Ukraine's resistance, culture, and people that they're learning Ukrainian.

Why is it thrilling to hear people speaking Ukrainian with an accent, making mistakes? The ability to assimilate new, imperfect speakers is a sign of a thriving, mature language, one with enough flexibility and generosity to take some "abuse." When somebody puts words together in an unconventional way (even if out of ignorance, the way my Ukrainian friends speaking English sometimes construct the most delicious phrases), it can be perceived as an innovation rather than a threat.

***

Don't get me wrong: I didn't like speaking Ukrainian as a kid. It quickly became the language I "had to" speak in certain situations: to my revered, strict grandparents, in Ukrainian Saturday school, during summer camp (under constant threat of scolding). My Ukrainian had no sense of humor. Jokes in my group of nerdy diaspora friends were based on translation: we were all bilingual, and translating the lyrics of a sentimental/brutal Ukrainian folk song into prosaic English was all it took to bring us to tears.

The territory of modern-day Ukraine has historically been home to many languages, including Ukrainian, Yiddish, Crimean Tatar, Russian, Polish, German, and *surzhyk* — a localized hybrid of Ukrainian and Russian. The capacity to adapt one's language to the surrounding context — whether at the scale of a reigning empire or a conversation between two people — is a Ukrainian talent that is often taken for granted by the people themselves.

Only after living for many years in Ukraine, discovering how much the language varies from region to region, did I suddenly wonder: how did the Ukrainian spoken in the North American diaspora — a specific version of early 20th-century western Ukrainian with some Polish, German, and even Ukrainian-sounding English thrown in — come to be one consistent language? If my grandmother grew up in a village in western Ukraine and her best friend in America was from the area of Ukraine that was part of the Russian empire, what transformations did their respective native languages undergo so that, by the time I was growing up in America, I learned their Ukrainian language? Did Ukrainian immigrants argue amongst themselves over which was the correct term for this or that? Did they make jokes about it?

Most of the best experimental contemporary art, performances, and discussions about culture in Kyiv circa 2005–2013 were happening in Russian. It's a language I learned unsystematically and incompletely through immersion, by listening to recorded lectures of Russian philosophers and by working for a few years with Russian art institutions. In Kyiv, my artist friends and I would read philosophical texts in English and Russian and discuss them in Russian (with me speaking Ukrainian). While we wrote our event announcements in Ukrainian on principle, we pondered why English or Russian lent themselves better to formulating our complex artistic concepts. Ukrainian felt a bit crude, lacking the nuance and sophistication for our subtle thoughts. Perhaps our Ukrainian was unsophisticated and underdeveloped compared to the languages in which we were respectively more fluent?

***

Ukrainian is enlivened by the power and energy of the people who use it. Their numbers jumped in the months following Russia's 2022 invasion, though it's been growing since 2014. Thinking in the Ukrainian language contributes to its discursive heritage. The connections between our experience as Ukrainians and the Ukrainian language grow sturdier with every intellectual debate, piece of writing, Facebook post, intimate conversation. This language is imbued with our early national aspirations, Soviet history, and the spunk Ukraine has demonstrated in wartime.

Today it is illegal, when providing emergency medical care to a wounded Ukrainian soldier, to speak Russian. If a victim wakes up hearing Russian, they may think they are in enemy hands and act rashly to protect themselves. It is a matter of personal and national security, like the passwords at checkpoints along major roads and entrances to cities throughout Ukraine designed to expose a Russian accent. "Slava Ukrayini!" is now declared all over the world. This concatenation of sounds conveys respect for those who fight for what they believe in and a wish for victory over evil.

A language is a common space, a place, formed by the speakers in the act of speaking it. Ukrainians' multilingualism, along with their talent for using different languages to fit various cultural contexts (think of Zelensky's near-daily video appearances in political halls around the world), certainly deserves admiration. But having your own language that you share with your people — knowing the language is the key to belonging to this group called "Ukrainians" — is fundamental.

Ukraine's defense has been so successful because of the mass participation of Ukraine's people, each contributing in their own way. The personal choice to speak Ukrainian is part of what creates the Ukrainian political nation fighting for its freedom, one that will endure long after its military victory. This is the language in which we will debate our cultural policy before writing it down in the official state language. When the language in which we are political coincides with the language in which we speak to our children and our friends, the individual citizens become the central driving life force of the nation. This is a powerful antidote to ideology, which still poses a great threat (encroaching from the Soviet past) to Ukraine's political existence.

Published in *Arrowsmith Journal* 21, December 2022.

Act III

Scene 1

In late September the Russian Federation is preparing to illegally annex about 15% of Ukraine's sovereign territory. Local occupation authorities in four regions of Ukraine hold referendums at gunpoint.

Russian officials vow to defend the Ukrainian lands they have claimed as Russian territory, insinuating that they could resort to using nuclear weapons if they are attacked.

The Ukrainian counteroffensive continues to advance and de-occupy more of its land.

On September 30 Ukraine's president Zelensky, on camera in Kyiv, signs an application for Ukraine's membership in NATO.

That same day, at an elaborate ceremony in the Kremlin, Russia declares the annexation of Ukraine's Luhansk, Donetsk, Zaporizhzhia, and Kherson regions – none of which it fully controls. In the following days, Russia's parliament votes unanimously to ratify the move and its president signs it into law.

The international community does not recognize Russia's claim.

October 3, 2022, Kyiv

I dreamt I was living in a house with Putin. That was my first thought on September 29. It was scary. We'd meet in the house in passing. I wanted to shoot and kill him. This is one of those actions that must succeed on the first try. But I was afraid he was out to kill me. It's the first dream I remember having since before February 24.

The sensation of being under attack, knowing that someone, an entire country and people, wants to destroy me, is real. The words and rockets emanating from Russia are a constant reminder.

***

Imagining the finality of a nuclear attack is tempting. It fills you with horror that floods the senses. You're practically paralyzed. Your stomach knots up and your mind is overwhelmed by fear. It's not unlike the sugar rush that stupefies you after eating an entire box of cookies in one sitting.

Living with the threat of nuclear attack is another story. In fact, if you survive the blast and the first hour and then the next 24, you have a pretty good chance of going on living. But it takes a bit of time to calm the nerves and start making preparations to survive.

You start packing your bag on September 29, the day before he's set to make the announcement,[29] which for all its fictitiousness will provide the "grounds" to justify a more brutal attack. Though a terrorist state needs no grounds or justification for its acts of terror.

Still you are pretty sure that the city you're in will not be subject to a nuclear attack tonight, and if you start getting ready now, when you have the time to fumble around and think spatially, you'll work some things out and be able to act more quickly the next time.

Rehearsing is important. Because you can't expect to think of everything on the first try. So you decide, yes, you will pack your

---

29   On September 30, amidst pomp and ceremony, Russia's president Putin announced the annexation of four regions of Ukraine, none of which is fully occupied by the RF.

bags for real, meaning close the computer, put it and the power cords in your backpack (I know a nuclear explosion will knock out electricity, but still, my computer is practically everything), accepting that you will have to take it out the next morning and repeat the same procedure every night . . . until . . .

Cool head. It's like packing for a trip. Something you've done countless times before. Something you've gotten really good at. You know how to live out of a backpack.

The threshold between imagining and action is personal. Crossing it is empowering. You grab a change of clothes and put it in your bag, along with a bottle of water, acetone nail polish remover, and a specifically Ukrainian detoxification substance called Enterosgel (that's helped you through many a hangover).

As you're walking around the apartment, the question at the front of your mind is: where will you go? It's so obviously ridiculous that you're packing a "go bag" with no clear idea of where you will go with it that you start to laugh. And this too is real.

Rehearsing for me is not about the future at all. It's how I stop my head from spinning into wild fantasies about what might happen by doing something concrete now. I don't need to know everything all at once. I just need to know what I will do tonight. And tomorrow, if I learn of a better option, I'll revise the plan. That's how we live now.

***

At night I open *The Black Book*, a thick volume documenting the Nazis' destruction of 1.5 million Soviet Jews, and read tales of who was killed and where, exactly 81 years ago in Nazi-occupied Kyiv.

> Sarra Evenson's advanced age and bad health did not permit her to be evacuated from Kiev. She had not left the house for two years. This great-grandmother was thrown from a third floor window at 14 Gorky Street.
>
> Regina Lazarevna Magat (10 Gorky Street), the mother of a professor of medicine and biology who had died at the front, was murdered by the Germans. The well-known lawyer Ilya Lvovich Bagat died from a German bullet along with his two grand-daughters, Polina and Malvina. Moisey Grigorievich Benyash, a professor of bacteriology known throughout the

Soviet Union and Europe, also perished in those days together with his sister and niece.

But all this was merely a prelude to later events which unfolded in the cruelest and most treacherous fashion in Babi Yar.[30]

I take comfort in the concrete facts, imagining each neighborhood. It's humbling to remember that my city bears a long, ugly history of genocide.

There is an excerpt from the diary of a woman who was rounded up in Mariupol for execution. She awoke under a pile of corpses; the Germans had done a sloppy job of killing the city's Jews at the edge of a defensive trench beyond the city limits. Sarra Gleykh crawled out and spent a month outdoors before finding a Red Army detachment. Her journal of the first days of the Nazi occupation, including the detailed recollection of her intended murder, survived. How did she hang onto it while being stripped and shot? She must have written it later from memory. Then did she leave her notebook behind and find it afterward?

So many stories I had heard about World War II make sense to me now. Including the vexing question of why Jews showed up with their belongings when called to collection points by the Nazi occupiers. "How could they have been so gullible?" I used to think from my 21st-century point of view. Now, even without direct experience of living under occupation, it's obvious how in dire, chaotic situations, you listen to the people with the authority to organize evacuations, distribute food, exercise deadly force, etc. Some people showed up to Babyn Yar[31] on September 29, 1941, expecting a labor mobilization or resettlement, or to be exchanged for German POWs and end up in Soviet territory. Other Jews did not heed the call to go to the ravine in northwest Kyiv. Some tiny sliver of them must have survived; the rest were found and killed anyway. At some point it's just a matter of luck.

***

30   "Kiev, Babi Yar," Lez Ozerov, in *The Black Book*, ed. Ilya Ehrenburg and Vasily Grossman, trans. John Glad and James S. Levine (New York: Holocaust Library, 1981), p. 6.

31   This is the transliteration from Ukrainian, while "Babi Yar" is from Russian.

There is no nuclear explosion in Kyiv on the night of September 29. On September 30 I sleep in and then turn on the news and learn that a humanitarian convoy of civilian automobiles outside Za-porizhzhia was struck by a Russian missile, killing 30 people (there were, of course, no military objects nearby). Another couple of missiles hit the center of Dnipro.

Morning on October 1 in Kyiv is glorious: vibrant with color, a bright blue sky, and the river without a ripple.

Scene 2

On October 8, 2022, a massive explosion destroys a section of the Crimean Bridge, which Russia had constructed – without Ukraine's consent – to connect its mainland with the Crimean peninsula it illegally annexed in 2014. The movement of military supplies from the RF is disrupted.

The RF begins a massive campaign of missile strikes on Ukraine's civilian and critical infrastructure, with a large-scale attack on October 10.

I am back in my Kyiv apartment. Performing old routines in entirely new conditions.

In late October Russia pulls out of the Black Sea grain deal, which had allowed for the safe movement of grain bound for world markets from Ukrainian ports that Russia is blockading.

Frequent Russian missile strikes, augmented by Iranian Shahed drones, continue into the fall, hitting major power stations and municipal heating facilities. Ukraine's ability to provide electricity and heat to its citizens throughout the country is greatly compromised.

On November 11 the Armed Forces of Ukraine reach the regional capital Kherson, freeing its people from Russian occupation.

October 23, 2022, Kyiv

When the power goes out (which has happened four times since October 10), it helps to be in my own apartment, where my body knows the routes from bedroom to bathroom, from kitchen to the hall, from years of repetition.

Despicable. Disorienting. Cowardly. Abhorrent. Undaunting. These words come to mind when I think about Russia's ongoing massive missile strikes on Ukraine's energy infrastructure throughout the country.

It makes life less pleasant (literally, colder and darker) but it also misses the point. Does life depend on my attachment to my iPhone?

***

Last night I danced. For the first time since mid-February I danced with abandon, relishing every moment of connection with my partner: coming closer, moving further away, getting lost, and then finding ourselves together again. The third dance with Vova was spectacular, and when he asked, "Shall we dance another?," I hesitated, knowing that agreeing to one more dance when I'm tired could destroy the magic that we've just created. "Yes," I replied, "as long as we take it easy." That reminder was more for me, with my partner as witness. We danced relaxed, loose, and when I caught myself trying to guess and match his lead I let go, which allowed me to actually feel where he was leading me and ease into it and just dance. Ah!

It felt incongruous to don so many layers in the dressing room before going home. I was—for once, this week—warm! And that warmth was still with me when I entered my cold apartment (even colder inside than outside!), stretched, took a warm shower, and then crawled into bed wearing a warm hat, nestling under three blankets.

***

I'm home again. In my beloved apartment in Kyiv. With the war right here in a visceral way. I've learned a new sound, that of an explosion in the air. It's a softer boom, could be mistaken for thunder. This is our air defense working successfully.

The glee as I stand in my kitchen, with the afternoon sun shining on the city's right bank across the river, is electrifying. And indecent. It is a kind of cruel happiness that knows that every missile and drone that was not struck down by Ukraine's air defenses *did* blow up something. And it wasn't me. It is not relief, but actual life force perking up and celebrating that I am here—and that *here* is intact—alive to enjoy this moment.

Unlike the historic apartment building a few blocks from Kyiv's main train station now in ruins. Or the flower market in the center of Mykolaiv. They now exist exclusively in the past, in somebody's memory; now some of those people who would remember them are gone too.

***

To start doing the things you used to do before February 24 means to reconnect with that past—memories of things done (or undone) and of moods, states of mind, habits of thought and feeling.

I've discovered two distinct selves: one that responds to outside stimuli and demands, who thinks and decides quickly what to do when she hears an explosion, gauging the distance, scanning the environment to assess whether it's better to stay put or move, and that acts on the most urgent needs that present themselves in the moment. Then there is that self with continuity, the one that remembers what I did or felt the other day, a year or even decades ago, the one with history, family, who is a member of communities and has relationships.

Perhaps in healthy, "normal" conditions, those two selves are one: you make decisions based on more complex considerations relating to the ways you are specifically tied to the world. But in the case of the emergency acting self, communities/relationships/memories of past experience are just resources for a more expedient response to and resolution of the immediate problem.

***

I find it strange and predictable when my friends write from abroad to check if I'm okay after Kyiv has been struck by missiles. That they care about my well-being is something I know regardless of when they write to me. That they write to me at this moment says more about the ways that our lives and imaginations are shaped by the news from the Internet and television.

Do you want me to reassure you that I am okay so that you can relax and go back to what you were doing? Do you want me to tell you what I see and smell out my window so you can get a more detailed picture of what's happening than what the news provides? Do you want me to tell you I'm scared and anxious and cold so that you can feel bad and commiserate? Is connecting with me an action that brings you closer to what is happening in Ukraine lest you feel helpless and overwhelmed by the barrage of news from your screens?

***

We need each other to share the pain and joy of living. Each person, with their distinct curiosity, touch, desire to reach out to the world and to another, all rooted in the body, is something more and separate from the schemes they use to think about the world around them. Humanism is an abstraction that substitutes an image of people who suffer but deserve comfort for people themselves, individual people in all their complexity. People are problems, always. Humanism wants to solve the problem of humanity once and for all.

What really matters to you? Playing with your kids? The smile of your beloved? Hugging a dear friend? These things are concrete (real). While the permanent safety of those people is an abstraction. Are you willing to give your life for an abstraction?

Pursuing abstract peace, abstract safety for abstract people, and the abstract idea "if Russia stops fighting" prevents you from seeing that Russia will not stop fighting. It must be stopped — by force, with weapons, through power, pressure, ruin.

In Ukraine we are fighting and dying for freedom. This may sound like a lofty ideal, but it is actually very concrete. It is freedom from being arbitrarily detained, tortured, raped, executed, deported at whim. But immediate dangers aside, it is freedom to live how we want to live. And how do we want to live? How do I want to live? Can you answer that question?

That is why I dance. Because in dancing—much more than in those hours alone in my cold apartment wracking my brain to figure out the logistics of getting seven Zippo hand warmers ordered on Amazon and then delivered to me in Kyiv relatively quickly—is where I am sharing the joy of being alive with others.

Culture is carried and reproduced through the body. There is no other way. It persists through our customs (food, rituals, dancing, and singing) and more broadly through the ways in which we relate to our environment and fellow human beings, in the ways that we construct and care for our world. Russia is trying to wipe out Ukraine as an entity, a concept, and a people through the total destruction of our homeland. That Ukrainians refuse to stop dancing, singing, and feeding their neighbors and defenders is one way of asserting ourselves as distinct and existing.

As my strength and vitality return, so does my sense of being in the world. Here the priority is clear: What did I do today to help Ukraine's armed forces?

Cuz all our culture and aspirations and dreams of a different kind of politics are nil if our army can't do its work and do it fucking brilliantly.

November 1, 2022, Kyiv

I started this letter-writing endeavor in March in a corridor in a borrowed apartment in Lviv. Now I'm writing in a cafe in my Kyiv neighborhood, but this too is a result of Russia's relentless missile strikes on Ukraine.

Yesterday I heard at least 10 explosions in half an hour around 8 AM. That the booms are soft and don't scare me just exhibits that Kyiv is a very big city. Some of them occurred in the air, but some definitely struck critical infrastructure.

In February Russia gathered its massive army, reputed to be the second strongest in the world, to invade Ukraine — this is an act of war, even though they call it a "special military operation." Now that the Ukrainian armed forces have staved off this attack for over eight months, Russia is aiming its missiles and Iranian drones[32] at Ukraine's energy infrastructure in an attempt to make the entire country unlivable.

These are NOT the army's supply lines. Nor the fuel, nor the ammunition our armed forces need to keep destroying enemy forces. No, these are power stations, water lines, train tracks, which ordinary people, all of us, depend on to keep moving. Movement is life.

The Russians failed to achieve their military objectives in Ukraine, so they're resorting to terrorism.

When Russia pulls out of the agreement to ensure the safe transport of Ukrainian grain from Ukrainian ports that Russia has bombed repeatedly, is it terrorism or an act of war?[33] What matters

---

32 Iranian-made Shahed-136 drones were first observed in use by Russia in Ukraine in mid-September. Bearing Russian markings, they have been used to attack Ukrainian military positions, civilian infrastructure, and to help locate Ukraine's air defenses and spend down their supplies. One Shahed-136 costs between $20,000 and $50,000. In response, Ukraine reduced its diplomatic relations with Iran, although the latter repeatedly denied supplying drones to the RF.

33 On October 29, 2022, the RF suspended indefinitely its participation in an agreement to ensure the export of grain from Ukrainian ports (blockaded by Russia). Earlier, in July, Ukraine and Russia had signed an agreement brokered by the UN and Turkey in which Russia pledged to unblock ports on the Black Sea to allow the safe passage of grain and oilseeds. According to CNN, "The World Food Programme estimated that tens of millions of people moved into a

is that you, in the West, understand that this gesture is addressing *you* directly. What you do and say and how you see it matters. In fact the future of our world depends on it.

***

I hear the morning explosions and acknowledge that they are nowhere near me. I am not in any immediate danger or suffering that requires action to survive. Still, I am in a city that is being struck by missiles (I don't know how many there will be or where they will land or how long this rain will last). We are creatures of our environment. And so I cannot go on in the same way that I would were the missiles not arriving, were the air raid alarm over or never begun. So. . . what? Where? I move and act in fits and starts. Sometimes I just pause in the kitchen and stand. Larissa, what is the most urgent thing that you need to do right now?

Listen to the news, check the Telegram chats to gather snippets of information about conditions in other parts of the city and country that the general news won't mention. Send notes to family abroad assuring them that I'm okay. Check in with friends. Chat a bit once we've established contact. I don't like being alone in war. Not because I'm scared or don't know what to do. But it seems like whether I'm alive or dead is irrelevant if I'm not in contact with anything living. In this situation the only thing that matters is to write. To send a signal toward the world.

This constant flux of unpredictable events—explosions, air raid alarms, repeated erratic power outages—makes it impossible to rely on anything. It defies the natural expectation that what is here now will be here in the next moment, that cycles of light and darkness will repeat in their established rhythms.

Life out of rhythm is bearable but disorienting. I suspect this is a test, challenging me to be more decisive. This is a war after all.

***

---

stage of acute hunger as a consequence of the Ukraine war" (https://edition.cnn.com/europe/live-news/russia-ukraine-war-news-10-31-22/h_208ece6b1614a78cb0973c794266d0fd).

The power goes out at 4:30 PM. The sudden plunge into darkness throws you from your habits. Even the streetlights, which have been blazing indiscriminately for the past few weeks, are out today.

It's jarring for the eyes to switch between the darkness of my room and the brightness of the screen in front of me. Or the patch of ground illuminated by headlights and the surrounding darkness with people moving through it. The number of pedestrians killed by cars in Kyiv over the past two weeks is 51% higher than usual.

Zelensky was right: I'm not afraid of the dark. And the darkness is nothing you can fight. It's a different condition, and my state changes to adapt, like any creature tuning to its environment.

Two and a half hours later the power returns. I've gotten used to losing power once a day for 2–3 hours. Of course you never know at exactly what moment it will happen or how long it will last. Today it went out twice.

My greatest fear is that the power will go out while I'm in the elevator. Sometimes I take the stairs (think of it as exercise) just in case. Other times I try my luck. So far so good.

Sitting at a café overflowing with people at their laptops, charging their devices, entangled in wires crammed into every visible outlet, I feel an ambivalent solidarity. We understand the Ukrainian electric utilities and government are working superhumanly to keep the country running, powered, connected. Nobody complains. Still, just grinning and bearing it, running my washing machine at 4 AM, is not going to win the war nor is it going to stop Russia.

These new attacks threaten my life in a different and possibly more insidious way than deadly fire, for this survivable disruption teases my body with the possibility of adaptation. Ultimately this is an expression of power. The ones with more missiles, with a greater supply of weapons, are in control. Am I a citizen fighting to live in my country? Or am I a slave surviving whatever conditions are set by the commander of the concentration camp?

In this moment, it is still up to me to decide.

November 13, 2022, Kyiv

The 7th floor is quiet after my climbing the stairs. No children screaming across the hall. No cat face — eyes flashing green in the dark — to greet me when I open the apartment door.

Now my life is structured by the schedule of rolling blackouts: 4 hours off, 5 hours on, 4 hours off... The schedule varies from day to day. Mondays, Thursdays, and Sundays are the worst: the power is off from 9 AM to 1 PM and again from 6 until 10 PM. If I have to go out to meet somebody in the afternoon, I have practically no chance to work at the computer with Internet access. Scrambling to finish my shower or an email that can't wait until tomorrow, I anticipate the impending power cut. But the abrupt change to total darkness is always a shock.

Sometimes it goes off off-schedule. It's confusing, too, when the power is on when I expect it to be off. Should I take it as a gift? Or a sign that they're repairing the power lines and soon these regular blackouts will stop (until the next missile barrage)? Maybe I don't have to think of a café or a friend's place to go to for my next Zoom appearance?

The other day found me in a dimly lit café, translating for an American psychiatrist consulting Ukrainian psychosocial support providers who work with people who've had to flee their homes. "When you're in survival mode," she says, "you don't have attention and energy available for planning ahead." I'm surviving alright, but in a mode with a similar effect: scrambled mode? scrambled eggs mode?? scrambled eggs à la mode???

It's taken a toll on my health and psyche. On my friends' too: each is a bit disoriented, more anxious, deeply tired. We reach for one another for support and yet each one of us is depleted, with nothing extra to give. My friend Larysa shares a piece of wisdom from her Japanese butoh teacher: when your mind is tired, enliven your body with spirit.

***

The morning light draws me outside. Walking along the river I look into the faces of people I pass. Hardship opens me to seek companionship. Sharing a kind word with a stranger might elicit one in return. Most of the faces are closed; some acknowledge my shy smile; others transmit an anguish that stops me from blurting out, "Good day!"

Civilian life in the midst of war is an uncomfortable exercise in contradiction. If being a warrior demands complete acceptance of the circumstances you are in to focus on how you can best perform your task right now, then the very actions and patterns of civilian life include a memory or residue of those peacetime conditions that are now missing. You may have no guarantee that the power or Internet will be available in the next moment, no assurance that the store or water fountain you've set out for will be working when you get there, but your life still consists of obligations that depend on these things.

And when you're working in a civilian framework with people around the world who do have electricity 24/7 and do not live under constant threat of missile strikes, then you too are supposed to be reliable. That's part of the unspoken agreement that underlies any commitment to work together: that you will do your part to overcome your unreliable conditions to show up on Zoom at the agreed-upon time and find in yourself the strength and clarity of mind to perform.

"Kyiv is functioning," I said to a roomful of Americans at a university in Connecticut (and some invisible viewers online) on Tuesday. Afterward I regretted that I chose to highlight Ukrainians' fortitude and resourcefulness in the face of adversity instead of giving them a more visceral picture of what it's like to live mostly in the dark.

One listener asked, "How can we help Ukrainians with electricity?" While the panelists from the Dnipro city council talked about generators, I wondered why this question made me mad. "Look, Ukrainians are coping and will continue to persevere," I added, "but the issue is not the number of generators we have. The issue we need your help with is making it impossible for Russia to keep hitting our critical infrastructure with missiles."

For all their genuine care and commitment, most Americans still treat what is happening in Ukraine as a misfortune.

***

The news that the Armed Forces of Ukraine have entered Kherson is amazing.[34] Watching the crowd in the city center cry "Kherson is Ukraine!" I have flashbacks to watching videos in March of the residents of that city newly occupied by Russian forces shouting "Kherson is Ukraine!" while the latter shot and sprayed gas at them. I am happy for the residents of Kherson that they are in Ukraine now. What does their return to freedom look like? People driving through the city honking their horns; leaving their houses to shout "Slava Ukrayini!" and "God bless you!" to the Ukrainian soldiers walking by; holding hands and dancing in a circle in the dark in the middle of the city square. Freedom means being able to act and speak according to how you are moved.

When you're watching the war from a safe distance it's tempting to fall into spectator mode. You're uplifted by every gain, by every brilliant maneuver. And when your guys lose, you go home disappointed. But your home is still there, just as you left it. And you can turn the lights on or choose to leave them off.

Walking along the dark streets of Kyiv one evening it hits me: the world that we've built—globally interconnected and interdependent—depends on us getting along in order to function. And this interdependence has reached a scale at which compromise between nations (or corporations) can threaten the freedom of people to take care of themselves and organize their lives together, in contact with one another at the scale of local communities (and sovereign nations).

When the war is happening onscreen, it's easy to exercise your logical reasoning in the privacy of your own mind and favor abstract solutions at a global scale or imagine ways to help alleviate

---

34   On November 11, 2022, the AFU liberated Kherson, the capital of one of the four regions Russia illegally annexed in October. After abandoning the city, Russian forces stationed nearby have continued shelling the city mercilessly and constantly, resulting in repeated civilian deaths.

suffering in the most effective way possible. It's only when you take a step to get involved that you hit upon physical realities — size and weight, distance and time, cost and mortality. Every logistical operation involves dealing with people and the systems they've created, varied and specific to every culture.

Kyiv, like many Ukrainian cities, still has citywide centralized heating. This is but one holdover from the Soviet Union's policy of centralized control over all aspects of life. Today Ukrainians are thinking about localizing energy production and consumption at the scale of building or neighborhood. While we fight to secure and protect the freedom to practice our own political culture, we in Ukraine also face a no less daunting challenge: noticing our own deep-seated Soviet attitudes toward power, control, and cooperation and refusing to perpetuate them.

***

One morning I hear a loud whistling as I walk through the park; it's intermingled with bird sounds, but distinctly human. On the way back home I pass the culprit and can't help but grin. He responds with traditional Soviet brusqueness: Whistling fortifies the spirit.

Scene 3

The days grow shorter and colder. Ukrainians are living with intermittent power, heat, and running water.

Russia is continuing its missile barrages nearly every week. A Ukrainian meme appears: ППОнеділок – a mash-up of the acronym for "Anti-Aircraft Defense" and "Monday."

I start practicing the Feldenkrais Method again. Once a week, as a volunteer, I teach "Awareness Through Movement" classes for wounded soldiers at a rehabilitation center outside Kyiv.

On November 15 the RF launches 100 missiles into Ukraine.

That day a missile strikes a village, just over the border, in Poland, killing two Poles. Members of the G7 meet in Bali (where they were already attending the G20 summit) to discuss what to do. NATO Article 4 is not invoked. The next morning's news carries stories claiming the missile was likely Ukrainian air defense that accidentally missed its mark.

Ukrainian emergency services and power crews work tirelessly to keep the country up and running. Working long hours out in the field, repairing damaged equipment and searching for people trapped under rubble, leaves them vulnerable to the ongoing missile strikes.

Ukrainians are undaunted – their disgust for Russia only grows.

November 23, 2022, Kyiv

This month I started going to a rehabilitation center for Ukrainian soldiers outside Kyiv to teach "Awareness Through Movement" on Wednesdays. They lie on the floor while I talk them through a series of movements for an hour, asking questions to direct their attention to sense with greater breadth and finer nuance what they are doing in any given moment. Today I failed to make it.

Until February 24 I was a Feldenkrais practitioner-in-training and taught classes like this a couple of times per week. It's best done in a quiet, warm room, as it's important to work in comfort and ease. Discomfort distracts your attention from sensing the details of movement and breath.

Last week I managed to teach three classes — two with a group of acting students and one with the soldiers. The cold creates a challenge, but one that is not impossible to overcome. Yesterday while preparing I found I could hardly move, in part due to all the clothing — sweater, hood, scarf — cluttering my neck and torso, in part from the condition my body is in — tense, gathered, like a bulwark against the cold and the unpredictable, constantly changing conditions. The light goes on, the light goes off, it comes back on again (oh, joy!).

***

On Saturday at home the power went on at 9:30 AM and didn't go off for the next scheduled blackout. It didn't go out in the evening and by 11 PM I was wracking my brain: What else should I scramble to do while I have power and Internet? What can I read? Who do I owe a letter? Can I just turn off the lights and go to bed? A sense of normalcy was returning; I could almost relax.

On Sunday I wake up to a stench of sewage in the apartment. It had been coming in periodically over the past weeks: I assumed it had something to do with the regular power outages; maybe some pumps in the building weren't working properly. But I noticed cracks in the ceiling near the sewage pipe in the bathroom, and another one in the hall from when I'd been flooded by the upstairs neighbors some years before. The crack continues into the next room, ending in a water stain, which appeared during that past accident but now looks like it's getting bigger.

Now I'm imagining that the sewage drainpipe is leaking somewhere between our two floors and dirty water is gathering in this space that is neither theirs nor mine and at any minute it will start dripping and then pouring down into my apartment. This is what I tell the building superintendent, a high-strung Soviet woman who does her job but not before telling you off, bemoaning how difficult her job and her life are and how much you've put her out by calling about the problems in your apartment . . .

"Nadia Mykolaivna, are you going to call the emergency plumbing service or should I do it myself?"

"Larissochka, have I ever let you down? Tell me, I've always done what you asked, right???"

"Yes. Please call the plumber and ask that he come today."

The plumber arrives in the late afternoon; it's getting dark, the power is out, but he's got his own flashlight. He pokes around the bathroom and asks when was the last time I used the small sink by the toilet. I don't use it.

"That's where the smell is coming from! When there's water in the siphon, the curved bottom of the drainpipe, it blocks odors from coming in from the main sewage pipe; if it dries out, then the smell comes in." He takes apart the pipe to check — dry as a desert.

"Really?" I gape at him. No sewage collecting above my head to burst through the ceiling at any moment?

"Trust me," he says.

"I'd be delighted if that's all! But I want you to take a look at the kitchen."

He listens to me patiently, as if he were talking to his wife. Lets me show him all the places in the apartment where I smell something funny. He takes the box of matches from the counter, lights one, and holds it up to the kitchen vent. "See that?" The flame is drawn toward the vent. "Nothing coming from there." I agree.

"But what about the cracks in my ceiling?"

"The cracks in the ceiling are dry. If there were something flooding from above they'd be damp." That's logical. I've already learned that the crack runs along the "fault line" where two structural panels meet. They form the floor of the apartment upstairs and the ceiling of mine.

"There's no space in between?"

"No space in between," he assures me.

"How much do I owe you for this visit?" I ask.

"Minimum charge is 350 hryvnias," he says, almost like he feels bad to charge me. I don't mind. This is what I needed: to talk to a man, and one who understands the construction of this building better than I do and how the water system works between apartments.

It's all a bit ridiculous, and I haven't completely let go of my nightmare fantasy. "Could you please leave your name just in case something happens in the next day or two and I have a question?"

When he leaves I'm unnerved. I was convinced — by the evidence of my senses and the story my mind constructed — that I was on the verge of being inundated by sewage from the upstairs apartment. The first thing he did when he entered the bathroom was to feel the sewage drainpipe. Dry. "If there were a leak, it would be dripping down along your pipe continuously. It's dry: no leak."

The cracks in the ceiling, the smells, the old wallpaper that's been peeling from the walls for years but drooped a bit more *this* morning... I was ready for the worst.

I just tape up the drain in the sink as he advised and really, the smell from there has stopped.

***

After talking to Dima from the rehabilitation center this morning about how to organize my Feldenkrais classes so that more soldiers attend, I had a feeling that maybe I should skip today.

The air raid alarm sounded 45 minutes before I planned to leave. When there's an air raid alarm the metro stops running to my aboveground station. But anything can happen in 45 minutes, so I sit down to lunch and stick to my original intentions. I'm getting ready to go and hear a bang when I'm in the bathroom. Was that an explosion? It could have been someone banging the door to the stairwell. Though why would they be in the stairwell if the power is on?

At 1:30 PM the alarm is still on and it's late to take an alternate route via public transport. How much will a taxi cost? It's affordable. And quick. When I get into the car I ask, "Is the air raid still on?" Yup. "Did you hear any explosions?" No. "I heard a sound, but it may have just been someone banging the door."

By the time we're driving through the center I'm having misgivings—should I go through with the plan?—and then I realize we're on the right bank. Here the metro is running—safely underground. I ask the driver to drop me off at the nearest station, pay him the full rate, and descend. There are people milling about the underground passage, near the turnstiles, sitting on the extra escalator that's not moving and scrolling their phones. While others descend and ascend, continuing their movements through the city.

I'm already behind schedule when the train unexpectedly stops one station before my destination. And waits there. And then announces that all metro service has stopped for the time being. By this point I've read that some critical infrastructure has been hit. And I've decided to abort my mission to go teach "Awareness Through Movement" to a handful of soldiers outside of town.

Because all this time I've been preoccupied with my movements about the city, with indecision, and not rehearsing my lesson. My attention isn't tuned. We're in another missile shower, we're being hit, mobile service is down, I can't get through to tell them I won't make it, and now the metro has stopped and I'm stranded at a station in a part of town I hardly know, and I feel the urgency of waning daylight even though it's barely 3 PM.

***

Sitting on the toilet in the dark, alone in my cold apartment, everything I've failed to do in the past decades comes back tenfold. It's not just missing a partner, lacking a life purpose, and that I still haven't insulated my balcony and windows. What did I not write, what questions did I fail to ask, when did I hesitate or chicken out, that I should be sitting here with Russian missiles raining down on my home while the good people of the world look on and yearn for some benign way to get out of this? Where is the political community of autonomous thinking individuals that *I* yearn for?

***

I'm resigned to the fact that the power won't come back on tonight, nor will the water return. But the sun will rise tomorrow, bestowing daylight upon us, of this I'm sure. And on December 22 the days will start growing longer and next spring it will start getting warmer. Nature is a great comfort with its cyclical rhythms.

I didn't realize I had such a strong attachment to the future until the lights started going out.

November 30, 2022, Kyiv

Evening. Walking home from the metro in the dark I wait for a handful of pedestrians to gather to cross the street. The traffic light at this busy intersection is off. Our clump of bodies forges into the street and the oncoming cars slow down, just enough to let us pass and then keep going. This negotiation happens in action: we don't spend time coming to an agreement through words or glances. Sure it's risky, but not scary. We used to depend on the traffic lights to direct our movements through this shared space; now it's a matter of personal timing, watching your surroundings, and trust. Shining a flashlight makes you more visible to the drivers; so does wearing reflectors.

I scan the buildings on either side of the road to see which ones have power (lots of lit windows) and which are out (only a few windows glimmer faintly from battery-powered lamps or candles). The hum of generators that keep cafés running has become commonplace.

While the city and country boast of "invincibility points" they've set up for people to warm up and charge their devices when there's no power at home, in fact most people — in typical Ukrainian fashion — find their own ways to cope. I've taken to working at cafés; my friends found a few tables in a neighborhood shopping center where there's wifi. The sort of self-organization where individual sharing (whether by people or businesses) meets individual needs remains more reliable than municipal "organized" solutions.

We're preparing for more attacks. Somebody said November 28, but that day and the next passed relatively uneventfully. Still I live in a dual mindset: one part anticipating conditions getting much worse and making plans for surviving, the other living from day to day, following my own priorities (what to write, who to see, when to dance) as long as nothing gets in the way. Sitting and waiting for Russia's next missile barrage is unconscionable.

***

The foreign journalists I talk to, seasoned war correspondents who've reported from Georgia, Iraq, Bosnia, marvel at the comforts of civilization one finds in Ukraine: delicious coffee on every corner in Kyiv, imported craft beer at the gas station on the way to Mykolaiv!

In cozy, elegant cafes, over flat whites, they give me practical advice from lived experience. Put each candle in a wine bottle: if you fall asleep, it will burn down into the bottle and not set your house on fire. A gas-powered heater with a vertical grille that projects heat into the room is better than one that warms the ceiling.

War correspondents are people with a surplus of curiosity, intelligence, and a thirst for adventure, who go somewhere else to see strife firsthand and report on it to the folks back home. In conversation it's easy to imagine I could be one too. But no: while I share the desire to be where the action is, I'm also very attached to my home.

Nine months of incessant Russian attacks on Ukraine, each day bringing the possibility of a countrywide blackout, and I'm having flashbacks to February: I just don't want to leave my home. It's a base, primal feeling (prior to being a political stance). Like an obstinate child who does not want to give up whatever is bringing them delight. Only there is nothing fun about waking up each morning to ask: Do I have power or not? What do I have to do most urgently that I can do in these conditions, before they change? I can stay because I'm not responsible for anyone else (not even my cat, who's still in Poland). I am responsible for maintaining my connection to my home and making this home livable. Here it becomes political.

***

Light brings a lightening of my mood as well as lightning-speed thought, moving from one action to the next. With darkness comes a slackening of spirits. It's easier to refrain from making an extra effort—to open the computer, to leave the house, to get up from the chair while the candle burns bright. That we humans are dominant over nature is a deadening fiction: in fact our life is always a struggle with our environment.

In February, amidst speculation that Russia could disable Ukraine's Internet and communication networks, I only dreaded the result without giving much thought to how it could happen. I used to consider things like artificial light and heat part of my environment, without knowing exactly how and where they were generated through specific mechanical (or nuclear) processes. A missile sent from Russia that hits a power station or transformer can cause enough damage to a system of interrelated, moving parts to leave millions of people without electricity.

My friend Sasha pointed out the similarity between the Ukrainian words for light (світло *svitlo*), holiday (свято *sviato*), and world (світ *svit*). In Russian there is no etymological connection: свет (*svet*), праздник (*prazdnik*), мир (*mir*).

Actually the Russian word мир (*mir*) means both "world" and "peace." This is fundamentally different, conceptually, from a world based on human political agency. The latter world requires *light* to illuminate the free (thus unpredictable) human action that is at the heart of political human existence, which is distinct but inseparable from nature and biological existence. Whereas *peace* is an abstract ideal.

It seems that abstract ideas and knowledge — the kind you've read, imagined, even thought through detached from personal, visceral experience — provide a sense of security. You think you "know" and thus have power. The impotence of Western people (which is not ultimate) comes from losing touch with or actively suppressing contact with concrete matter, with what is really happening. As long as individuals and their political bodies live in dreams and projections, privileging their fears of (or enchantment with) those imaginary images, they remain powerless to fight Russia and actually empower it to keep waging war against the world of light.

***

Monday I climbed the stairs to the 14th floor to spend a few hours in my friends' dim kitchen discussing renting a house with a wood-stove for the next couple of months. How much water would we need in bottles in case the power goes out and the pump from the well stops working? How much does it cost to buy a generator; and is it better to buy a small one or one that is a bit more powerful; which will be more efficient? Where will the three of us sleep if the woodstove heats only the first floor? Yes, it's worth investing a few hundred dollars to have a place available in the event the city heating system fails.

My friend calls the next day to say the owners decided to rent the house to somebody else. We're back almost where we started, though it was worth starting to think about this more concretely. "By the way, do you have power?" No, she says. And just as I'm about to invite her to come share ours I see that it's gone out too. I can do nothing but laugh, verging on hysteria, but really, it's funny.

The waning daylight brings insight: I used to think that you go to the place of action to gain experience. To see with your own eyes, to smell, hear, sense, be moved by moving around in it. Ah no, it's *far* more humbling. You go and get embroiled in reality to meet your own limitations.

Heroic acts are visible from afar. When you surpass your own limitations, glory shines through. But every day of ordinary life — including when you're living through history — is just that: deeply humbling. You can't always be exceeding your limitations. And yet you still have to be ready to at any moment.

December 12, 2022, Kyiv

Three hours of electricity today. Three hours and 23 minutes, to be precise (until nighttime). I've started keeping a log. Usually it's around 6–8 hours, split between a couple blocks. Yesterday my friend called just as the evening blackout started. We took a long walk in the dark and drizzle through my puddled neighborhood. This raised my spirits.

***

Last Monday I packed up my computer and headed for my trusty café (which always has power) on the right bank to get some work done before meeting friends in the evening. Halfway through my coffee the air raid alarm sounded. The café is on the first floor of a five-story brick apartment building; the windows are small. I keep typing.

After a while the waitress comes up, agitated, and asks me to pay: they've decided to close up and go to the nearest bomb shelter. Some 70+ missiles are on their way. I close my laptop quickly and figure I'll do the same. Outside people walk with purpose, and many are clustered near the entrance to the underground metro station. Some stand around smoking or talking on the phone; it seems like everyone is receiving information from their telephones. I watch the people, wondering how soon the missiles will arrive, and decide in which direction to move if I hear one in the next instant.

In the underground passage sellers of fruit, cookies, and underwear continue their trade as people mill around. The metro entrance hall is also full of people. A few have taken positions near stone barriers that provide a good surface for a laptop. People continue arriving and descending via escalator to the platform below.

They cluster by the walls and columns along the whole length of the platform. The well-prepared have come with folding chairs, bottles of water, and snacks. Couples snuggle on ground pads or open their laptops side by side. I wonder if I'll find the USB charging stations promised by the Kyiv municipal Telegram channel.

"Attention! The air raid alarm has sounded. The metro station is serving as a bomb shelter. Trains are running on abridged routes." This sounds over the loudspeaker periodically as trains arrive, discharging and taking new passengers.

I need to write a Facebook post to tell people about the Feldenkrais class I plan to launch on Friday. "Awareness Through Movement in the Midst of War." There's an empty patch of wall that I can prop my back against while squatting to make a surface for my laptop. At least I'm not in a hurry.

When it's time to post my computer finds a network called "WIFI.METRO," but I can't actually open any websites. Strolling up and down the platform I even spot a router with lights flashing, but standing nearer or further away from it changes nothing. I can, however, get a connection on my mobile phone.

Retype the text from my laptop into my phone, choose an appropriate photo, and hit POST. Then sit and stare at the black screen until "Shared to Facebook!" appears. The post ends with a note in parentheses: this post was composed and uploaded from a metro platform serving as a bomb shelter during an air raid alarm.

***

My parents in the US kindly invite me to stay with them for as long as I want. They're visibly baffled that I should choose to stay in cold, dark Kyiv when they've got a cozy fireplace in Connecticut. It sounds more like a proposition to go back in time. To go back to a time when I am a child and my parents can protect me from the dangers of the world.

My parents cannot protect me from Russia. Rather, they can't protect me alone. This is why I get mad when people offer refuge instead of weapons. You can only protect me from Russia by fighting Russia. And then you are also protecting yourself from Russia and all of us from Russia. And isn't that a more virtuous aim than gathering the people you like and trying to maintain that "everything is okay" until it *really* isn't anymore?

Maintaining my sanity takes a lot of time and effort these days. As does being patient and kind with others who try my temper, for

I understand that everyone here is making enormous efforts to maintain their sanity.

***

On Sunday night, in a moment of electricity, I dash off an email to my Feldenkrais teacher in the US. I need help creating and structuring a program of "Awareness Through Movement" lessons for my rehabilitating soldiers. The group is diverse, ranging from one guy who is visibly bored to one recovering from a serious head injury that had him in a coma for a while, and for all of them this practice is new and weird. I'm in a panic because I have years of audio and video recordings from my past training in the computer and online, but little time with electricity and minimal desire to lie on the floor in the cold and just try things out. I need direction.

A few days later my teacher replies, offering a bunch of materials from his own recent classes in an online library. Elated to receive a response, in a brief moment with power I quickly write, "Thank you!!" and decide to look more closely tomorrow.

The next morning my mind is sharper and less generous: what sort of help is this, sending a person with a power deficit a wealth of video material *online*? What am I supposed to do with it? How can my friends abroad, with all their comforts of civilization, be so insensitive to the conditions I now live in?

But the power is on when I get up, so I quickly scan the lesson titles from the series he sent and choose one that catches my eye and download it. Remarkably the power stays on for six hours uninterrupted, which means the heating too. I lie down on the floor to do a lesson from a recording online, knowing full well that it might be interrupted at any moment. But it keeps going, alternating between movement and rest, and when it reaches the end and I'm awaiting the familiar "roll to your side, sit up, and then stand" the computer goes silent. As if according to plan! The lesson I grabbed from my teacher's online library was just what I needed for the week's classes (including the one I launched from the metro bomb shelter).

There is a moral here: Timing matters, and so does hitting your mark. The *how* is deeply personal, and we should honor other people's liberty to move in their own way. Listening and hearing are a matter of trust (which can be fortified or broken through action). There are always so many unforeseeable factors in play.

***

Today I got a battery-powered radio. It's almost as good as a fireplace.

December 23, 2022, Kyiv

Wake up, flick the lamp switch: no power. Under three blankets it's toasty warm. The air in the room is 12°C. Generators stutter outside every other storefront. Their noise pollutes the air; so does their exhaust.

The coffee shop near home is open, but not sharing power or wifi. Turn away from the gorgeous brownies on display and move on. The vegetarian café near the metro where I've spent many hours this month is warm — and crowded. Before placing an order I scan the dining room: every outlet is taken. I'm starving, but the priority is charging my devices and getting online.

Outside the day is sunny and mild. My trusty café on the right bank is without power. The air raid alarm in the city is the least of my concerns. For an hour I am a dejected nomad: hungry, directionless, and disconnected.

Then suddenly I am a "normal" person, sitting at my laptop in a hipster café, energized by rock music plus a flat white and sumptuous croque madame (pricey by Ukrainian standards is still less than $10 USD). The coffee shop (with power strips and extenders in every outlet) is packed with young, fashionable people, their dogs and devices.

In the 1930s Soviet Ukrainian intellectuals lived well in Kharkiv while the peasants in the surrounding villages were being starved to death. Today in Kyiv you can wake up in an apartment with no heat, electricity, or running water and spend the afternoon catching up on email while sipping aromatic coffee. Only the latter is getting more difficult by the day.

Lately I'm lucky to get 2–3 hours per day on the computer with power and Internet. You have to think quickly to work through everything that needs to be communicated online that day. Sometimes I just open Facebook or the *Guardian* and stare at the screen.

Invincibility is the stuff of myths and children's cartoons. In Ukraine it's beginning to show its cracks.

***

It's insidious to kill through conditions, the way Russia is trying to wage war by making Ukraine unlivable for everybody. Struggling with your environment is a part of survival. But the environment is not your enemy. Fighting or killing it would also involve destroying yourself. Confusing the enemy with the environment muddles your thinking, which plays into the enemy's hands.

Russia can't break us by attacking our "civilizational" infrastructure, because citywide electricity and heat is *not* our environment. It felt like it was in more peaceful times, but these are merely the specific solutions we collectively take to support our urban living together (primarily relying on the infrastructure left over from the Soviet period, without giving enough thought to its efficiency). Yes, it hurts to lose this and to suffer the resulting more direct encounter with one's winter environment (that I, for one, am not really equipped to handle alone). But we must also fight to not get lost and to not lose ourselves in these new conditions.

***

In the morning the room is cold, but a flick of the lamp switch shows that the power is on. You need to do everything right away — the moment you realize that the conditions are right. In this case, for taking a shower. Of course you can boil a pot of water on the stove and wash by candlelight, but it will be colder than when you have heat and can also steam up the room with hot running water. Did you know that you can dry your hair over a gas burner on the stove (make sure you stand on a chair, keeping your head far above the flames) if there's no power for your electric hair dryer?

The Kyiv municipal Telegram channel shows that there was an air raid alarm overnight—a long one. And then another in the morning. And some critical infrastructure was struck on the other side of the river.

My friend is supposed to give me a haircut at noon, and I write to check if we're still on. Yes, he replies. And then: "The salon just wrote that they don't have power. Can you wash your hair at home?"

I check the faucet, still running warm in the dark, before replying: Yes.

He did not even suggest that we cancel or reschedule, just spelled out the situation and offered a way to deal with it. The salon's front wall is a row of glass windows, so there's plenty of daylight to snip by.

"What are we doing today?"

"I want a wartime haircut."

"Oh no, that's too short!"

"Of course, not a buzz cut—I could do that myself!" I'm laughing. "Something shorter, cuz it's cold and I want less hair to dry in the winter. I won't wash it more than once a week, but I still wanna look pretty."

***

Russia is pounding away at civilization, turning the areas it ostensibly wishes to embrace (through illegal annexation) into rubble, transforming places that once were alive, including Ukraine's fertile black soil, into dirt and dust and minefields.

You are watching this destruction from afar. You can keep up with the news because you have power and Internet; it's probably warm enough for you to sit still with your phone or computer and imagine the horrors that Ukrainians are enduring. The war in Ukraine is part of your media environment. You struggle to keep the constant flood of information from inundating your attention or messing with your emotions. But you control the time you spend looking at your phone, checking the news. It's in your power to create a more "healthy media environment."

It's also in your power to shape the world in which the war is happening and to influence the outcome of the war.

The war in Ukraine is not a natural disaster. Russia is arguing that Ukraine belongs wholly to it and is trying to prove that Ukraine is a concentration camp by *concentrating* its missile barrages (except for that close call with Poland last month) and genocidal efforts on the territory and people within Ukraine's 1991 legal national borders. By contrast, Ukrainians are proving in battle that our freedom and right to govern ourselves are more than nice ideas. Our resistance itself is an expression of our freedom, and our fierce fighting protects our right to organize our lives together at this very moment, even in the midst of war. These two positions — Ukraine's and Russia's — are absolutely irreconcilable. And which position will prevail will be decided by a fight to the death.

In a recent interview with the *Economist*,[35] General Valery Zaluzhny, commander in chief of the Armed Forces of Ukraine, said, "Russians and any other enemies must be killed, just killed, and most importantly, we should not be afraid to do it."

This is no easy task (and I'm not just talking about being a good shot). I imagine the Ukrainians I know — dancers, entrepreneurs, leftist activists, historians, etc. — who enlisted in February and March. You sign up for the Armed Forces to defend your home and your people from attack, not because you want to kill people.

If you want Ukraine to win you have to accept the will and effort and work to destroy the enemy. If you want to not hurt Russia you will not be able to support Ukraine.

"We have already realised through a number of operations that the main thing is not to be afraid of this enemy. It can be fought, it must be fought today, here and now. And in no way should that be postponed until tomorrow, because there will be problems," said Zaluzhny.

Thinking as an American, I wonder: Does our support for Ukraine come from considering Ukraine and its freedom-loving will to self-government to be like our own? Or do we engage because we consider Russia and its great culture and imperial heritage and even the murderous Soviet experiment part of our own world history? Is this the moment when the US takes responsibility for its own role in shaping 20th-century Europe?

***

I've lost the sense of perspective that stretches into the future. It's as if the time in which things happened is in the past. My friend

---

35   Interview on December 3, 2022: https://www.economist.com/zaluzhny-transcript.

said she feels like there's not enough time to get into whatever is going on these days: it feels like it isn't real. I get what she's saying, but I know this *is* real, that this is *it*. There really is no time and you can't relax.

You do it now, or you don't and you have to live with the undone. It will be on your conscience, only you won't actually have time to think about it because you'll be dealing with the consequences.

Scene 4

New Year's Eve. I'm alone at home. At midnight (past curfew) the city is silent. A dog barks somewhere across the river. Someone sets off a few il-legal fireworks in the distance.

Then voices ring out in the neighborhood: Glory to Ukraine! Glory to the heroes! Glory to the nation! Death to the enemies!

Shortly after I climb into bed the missiles arrive. Of the 20 sent by Russia to usher in the New Year, one explodes in the sky just over my neighbor-hood.

Scene 5

The first days of 2023 grant permission to take a break.

I am compelled to get out of Kyiv. Plans to visit Poland fall through.

The apartment in Lviv where I took shelter in the first months after Russia's full-scale invasion is open. The power almost never goes out there.

Lviv is gloomy. The rattle of generators reverberates through narrow cobblestoned streets. Friends I had wanted to see are unavailable.

I am not the only one exhausted beyond my wits' end.

On the "old New Year," according to the Julian calendar, Russia launches a missile into a residential building in Dnipro, killing 46 and injuring nearly 80.

January 15, 2023, Kyiv

Many years ago, I went to visit a Ukrainian friend who was studying for her PhD on a meager Ukrainian university scholarship. She lived in a dormitory far from the center of Kyiv in one room with two other women, plus occasionally the boyfriend of one of them. It was a long walk from the metro, and after spending several hours in these spartan conditions it was time to leave. Upon parting she gave me a jar of honey her mom had sent her. I was moved by the gesture.

Like many Americans, I ration out my generosity and always keep something for myself in reserve. I am generous when I can be, as much as I can, because I can.

I grew up in the US with its "can do" spirit, believing that I really could do or be anything, if I put my mind to it and worked hard. Only this "I can" often stands in ignorance of actual material facts—from the specificity of your physical body to events that are happening around you to the challenges posed to your freedom by the people with whom you share your life and world. "I can" has no power when it doesn't acknowledge its flip side: "I could not."

True generosity—as a principle—is about sharing rather than giving away your surplus. It is about including the other—and whatever they offer you or ask of you—in your life. Just because they are here.

***

I went to Lviv for a change of scenery, greedy for warmth and uninterrupted electricity, and to recharge and come back to myself. It was just after New Year: I could take a break from the war. On vacation in Lviv, detached from my friends in Kyiv, instead of peace I encountered old habits and states of mind I thought I had left in the past.

In a moment when I was feeling overwhelmed, a dear old friend reached out to me asking for help. It touched a nerve and some personal history, and instead of taking the time to think and broach a difficult conversation with her, I put my own feelings first, acting from a place of cowardice, and simply refused to help. Because I could.

I was operating from my American mindset, which clearly separates me and my responsibilities from the responsibilities of another. So what if I don't help? I have other problems. Can't she just ask somebody else? Blinded by emotions rooted in the past, I missed the significance of being called upon to do something.

War is unforgiving. Your action shows who you really are. My capacity to ignore a friend's request for help betrays that somewhere in the back of my mind I still think that I can sequester myself from the demands of living through Russia's assault on Ukraine. My cowardice is like that of Americans who admire Ukrainian heroism without seeing that these Ukrainians are ordinary people, just like us, only they have nothing to fall back on, no corner in which to hide from the harsh choice between stopping Russia's invasion or being annihilated.

***

Ladies and gentlemen, it's time to grow up.

You think you've matured, you're learning to listen to your sensations and be true to what they tell you. You notice a conflict of interest and you take some time to think it through.

And then all of a sudden you don't. You are swept up in some old emotional habit, jealousy, feeling left out—a truly childish state of mind—and instead of recognizing it and taking some time to think, you act rashly and destroy a friendship of 15 years.

Now, ladies and gentlemen, before you gasp, "I'm so sorry!," let's be real: this is wartime.

And all that self-development and therapy and striving to be your better self . . .

Well, guess what, war catches you unprepared, the way that you are. And after nearly 11 months, when you are ragged and worn down and so is every single person around you, your ugliest comes out.

And sometimes that ugliest meets the ugliest of a person who has played a very important role in your life and something dies.

Not you, not the other person, but whatever trust or affection there was between you.

You only get one shot, one chance, and when you fail to think (no matter the reasons) the consequences can be deadly.

Ladies and gentlemen, welcome to real life.

***

I've told you about my Ukrainian grandparents. My grandfather was marked for murder by Polish insurgents and so they made a plan with their friends to flee westward in the middle of the night. Only my grandfather had an intuition that it was better to wait until morning to leave.

Next day my grandparents saw their friends, who had left at night, lying murdered by the side of the road.

Did my grandfather tell his friends about his intuition to wait? Did they argue about it and reach different conclusions? Or was he unable to get a message through? Or did he just decide it was too late or too risky to try to contact them and simply didn't show up as planned?

I'm here today because some people before me were really good at saving their own skin.

***

Isolation is tempting. If you don't have friends, then you won't see them dead, lying by the side of the road. If I don't forge connections, if I don't take on responsibilities, can I remain free? Am I more comfortable holding onto the dream of desired connection than doing what is asked of me as a participant in a relationship?

Instead of seeing the seriousness of my friend's request and the need for me to address it directly, I chose to view it as an abstract problem, thus securing my right to act "freely" according to my own wishes. I hurt her deeply and destroyed something that was a fundamental part of my life.

There is something similar in the way the Western world is treating Russia's brutal invasion of Ukraine. It is easier to protect your own reserves, to keep working toward an imaginary peace, to think the war is not your problem, than it is to face the monster that is threatening to destroy the world while its forces seem focused on a distant land.

When the US states a commitment to support Ukraine "for as long as it takes," it begs the question: As long as it takes . . . for what? For Ukraine to defeat Russia? Or for Ukrainians to tire and concede to a peace settlement? Or for Ukraine to be completely destroyed?

The challenge facing each Western person, myself included, is to see what is right before your eyes and to meet it head on. Pretending it doesn't concern you will have devastating results.

Epilogue

My mind these days is a jumble of what I've done, who and what I owe, and what is going on right now. My body is in Kyiv. My cat is in Poland. My family is in the United States. My friendships are in the past or in neglect.

My computer and phone provide access to nearly everyone I've ever met or ever could. But the real action is to the east and to the south. This is where we cannot fail.

***

I managed to call my grandmother this year on February 24 to wish her a happy birthday. True, it was evening when I remembered. But I was at home in my Kyiv apartment, free to sing "Многая літа"[36] over the phone from the comfort of my kitchen.

Earlier in the day, President Zelensky gave a press conference to a roomful of journalists from around the world. Two hours and fifteen minutes in, a Ukrainian journalist asked, "How have the last 365 days changed your relationship with your family, with your nearest and dearest?"

Here is a man whose face is lined, tired, so different from the boy in a suit who addressed international leaders at the Munich Security Conference in February 2022. That was before he made the now-historic decision to remain in Kyiv as Russian forces pushed toward the capital, before he saw the human wreckage those Russian forces left in Bucha and other Kyiv suburbs when the occupiers were cleared out at the start of April.

"It's important not to let them down," he says of his family. "It's important that my children be proud of me." They are in Ukraine, he says, in their own country, where Ukrainian boys and

---

36 *Mnohaya lita*—which literally means "many years" in Ukrainian—is traditionally sung in the Ukrainian diaspora on birthdays, anniversaries, weddings, and in any situation that invites collective celebratory affirmation.

girls are dying. They're studying at Ukrainian schools (a fact worth noting, as the post-Soviet elite usually send their children abroad to get an education).

The only thing I want to say exactly one year after Russia's full-scale invasion is "Thank You" to the Ukrainians: to the armed forces, the president, and the countless citizen-defenders fighting tirelessly every day, supporting the army and one another, reminding the world that Ukraine's fight and victory matter.

***

At this point any person I meet in Ukraine—at a live music show, in the museum, especially if they are involved with war work, but really anybody—has likely lost somebody (friends, coworkers, neighbors, loved ones) or parts of their own body to Russian fire, mines, missiles. Sobering, no?

But Ukrainians have been damaged for generations. You will not find a family without personal stories of violent arrest, deportation, unnatural death, or forced resettlement. People are more reluctant to talk about family members who committed these acts against their fellow citizens. I can attest that being uprooted from your homeland under the duress of war, refashioning yourself in a new land amongst new people in a new culture and language, leaves scars that last for generations. Soviet Ukrainians were severed from their land through collectivization, deportation, and forced resettlement—violent policies their own government devised to subordinate human life to an abstract ideal—without even leaving their country.

Ukraine's current battle against Russia's unjustifiable military invasion takes power and legitimacy from the success of Ukrainians in 2014 in resisting and ousting their corrupt government, which put the interests of Russia above those of its own citizens. Since then Ukrainians have been learning and practicing self-defense and self-government in an ongoing trial by fire (feel the difference between this and the controlled conditions of "trial and error"), building the networks that are now equipping and supplying military units, distributing humanitarian aid, rallying international support, and holding the current government accountable for its actions. The spirits and memory of the hundreds of thousands who have died in this fight do not allow us to give up.

***

US president Biden's appearance in Kyiv on February 20, honoring the nine-year anniversary of Ukrainians' resistance to subjugation,[37] differs from previous historic visits of American leaders. Strolling through central Kyiv during an air raid alarm, standing side by side with, or embracing, Ukraine's president Zelensky in this country that is reminding the world what protecting freedom and doing democracy require, the US president looks humble.

Anyone who's been watching the Ukrainians' ongoing valiant fight to secure their land and people from Russia's assault over the past year—while bearing tremendous loss—and watching the Americans' enthusiastic but circumspect support cannot help but see a difference. It's the contrast between generous sacrifice that cannot be called selfless and a cautious struggle to do what is right while maintaining the security of one's own position.

I respect Biden for coming to this place where he can only appear humble, even vulnerable. It's not a sign of the weakness of US power or influence in the world, but it does serve to remind us of those forms of power that come from principle, courage, and virtue, which are very much worth defending.

***

37 The 2014 Maidan protests reached a climax on February 18–20, when riot police, loyal to the pro-Kremlin Ukrainian government, began firing live rounds at protesters. Snipers stationed on rooftops shot and killed protesters on the street below. Of the "heavenly hundred" Maidan protesters who gave their lives, 48 were killed on February 20 alone. The following day thousands of riot police left Kyiv; the protesters gained power over the city and its government buildings, along with the support of the military. That evening the then president, Yanukovych, fled the country. On February 22 Oleksandr Turchynov was elected speaker of Parliament and acting president.

Wrapping up our conversation on Zoom the other day, my mother wishes me well, then adds, "and that we send you more artillery soon." At the word "artillery" I suddenly smile—spontaneously and sincerely (something I haven't done in a long time). This word was hardly part of my vocabulary a year ago.

Backstory:
Three Essays on Theater

Before Ukraine captured the world's attention by taking up arms against a formidable foe, its artists were grappling with fundamental questions: How can we live/work together while respecting one another's autonomy? What does it mean to be a citizen and participate in self-government? How do you take responsibility for your country's past? I spent over a decade mingling with some of Ukraine's most thought-provoking contemporary artists and performers in an intense milieu where personal and professional relationships overlapped and intertwined. Sometimes I was co-curator of an event or exhibition; sometimes a casual co-conspirator, chatting over beer on a park bench; sometimes I formally wrote about my experiences of artworks as a critic.

My encounter with contemporary performance art in Ukraine was first of all an education — learning how to see and think with the whole body. Here I met the works of philosophers Merab Mamardashvili, Alexander Piatigorsky, and Hannah Arendt. I practiced observing myself looking at an artwork, and from there examining the specific position I occupy — in the theater, in my political community, in the history of my country and the world. In post-Soviet Ukraine contemporary art was encouraged (i.e., funded) as an integral part of an open, democratic, free-market society. Recognizing the political power of artistic expression, my colleagues interrogated the relationship between freedom and responsibility in their work.

The following essays were published between 2015 and 2018. After Russia's undeclared incursion into Crimea and Ukraine's eastern regions, Ukrainians faced the urgent need to respond. At the same time, they had to face the fact that they hardly knew one another. While fighting to maintain their sovereignty, Ukrainians were scrambling to figure out who they are and what they stand for.

TanzLaboratorium's documentary theater project Expertyza offered its participants a way to appear before one another, to get to know coworkers and compatriots, and to practice speaking politically. This artwork, which resembled a structured public discussion, premiered in summer 2013, and was recreated dozens of times around Ukraine over the following years. This included traveling to cities that had been temporarily taken over by "separatists" in 2014, and inviting residents to express their views on citizenship, their personal values, and their thoughts about Ukraine. My essay for Springerin opens with a 2015 performance in Mariupol, *which had become a haven for people who fled Donetsk after Russia-backed separatists took control.*

As theater critic of The Odessa Review, *I wrote about the challenges of publicly addressing Ukraine's complex past through art. The 2017 Kyiv production of* The Trials of John Demjanjuk: A Holocaust Cabaret, *which I reviewed, put audiences in the uncomfortable position of judging someone who survived decades of brutal political violence, and who could have been both the victim and the perpetrator of unspeakable atrocities. Discussing the darker pages of Ukraine's history is also at the heart of my review of Mayhill C. Fowler's book* Beau Monde on Empire's Edge: State and Stage in Soviet Ukraine. *While introducing the legendary figures of Ukraine's 1920s theater scene to international scholarly discourse as ground-breaking artists, the author also studies their role in building the Soviet Union, whose ruthless regime murdered them a decade later. Reading Fowler's historical account while reflecting on my personal experience working with Ukrainian contemporary artists in the 2010s reveals similarities between the two artist–activist milieus working nearly 100 years apart. Both communities were driven by a desire for revolutionary change based on visions of a future that involved breaking from their past. Losing sight of your own history and keeping it out of public discussion practically guarantees its repeat performance.*

Playing at Politics, Learning to Speak

"We are the same kind of people as you!" cried one woman from the stage in Mariupol, replying to the frustrated criticism of an audience member. "You could have been here!" she said, indicating that their positions on either side of the "fourth wall" were interchangeable, determined not by special privilege or expertise, but almost arbitrary, based on voluntary response to an open call. The performance of the documentary theater project *Expertyza* in Mariupol last spring ended with the audience physically splitting along two sides of the auditorium—those who considered the experimental performance a complete "bomb," and those who did not.

This argument that ensued at the close of the show was already integrated into the work's structure: each performance ends with a period when audience members are invited to pose questions to the participants on stage. It highlighted the conflict between the social and political; between audience expectations that theater should "do something to them" in exchange for a ticket purchased, and "emancipated spectatorship," where the audience is offered a common experience to consider from individual positions; between teaching another person how to do something "right" according to what you know, and provoking someone else to think more deeply by taking an interest in his/her words and by offering your own questions.

Kyiv-based performance group TanzLaboratorium (TL) has been repeating the documentary theater work *Expertyza* (a Ukrainian word meaning "expert analysis") in different sites (a traditional black-box theater, army bases, museums, a church, etc.) since spring 2013. The project began at Les Kurbas National Theater Arts Center in Kyiv at a time when its employees were divided over the institution's future—as a way for them to get to know one another on the personal level (what do you like to eat for breakfast?), as colleagues (how do you envision the institution you would like to work in?), and as citizens (what form of government do you consider most agreeable?). *Expertyza* uses simple but precise rules to organize a discussion among voluntary participants, who perform as "experts" on their own life experience.

Eschewing the customary artifice used to represent reality on stage, these "rules of the game" create a sliver of space-time that allows one to examine autonomous elements and events as separate things. Members of an institution, community, or social category become visible as individual people; the words spoken appear as objects for analysis on stage and afterward. Evolving together with the changing social and political situation in Ukraine, the project has expanded to address a variety of pressing issues (including the Maidan protests, cultural policy, war and peace, discipline, and internally displaced persons and refugees). Since 2015, the artists have been traveling to towns all over Ukraine, including those along the border with the territory now occupied by the Russian army and Russia-supported local militias, and have sought to initiate conversations with and among local residents.

Recent performances have revealed that many people do not envision a world that allows for difference, or for anything that is not already accounted for in their existing worldview. (Perhaps this is one of the reasons that the 2013–2014 Maidan protests — which unleashed new kinds of cooperation and coexistence that defied my own capacity to describe or conceptualize them as they were emerging in action — were so quickly relegated to memory and official commemoration as a historical event, rather than as transforming, ongoing political processes.) Participants in all parts of Ukraine have repeatedly referred to others who are different from them as in need of correction, as potential members of society on the condition that they change their views or practices to align with the values of the speaker, or as "not normal."

In a village in the Carpathian Mountains, in western Ukraine, the conversation reached an impasse when one man declared that Ukrainians could unite only once everyone embraced the Christian faith. His conversation partner asked how they could live in the same society if his view did not allow for anyone other than Christians. Rather than considering a society where people do not impose their religious views on one another, he preferred to put off thinking about how Ukrainians could live together until religious unity was achieved. In Mariupol, under the auspices of *Expertyza*, a discussion without a formal audience was organized with female university students. When the question of single-sex romantic love was raised, the girl speaking said, "That's not right." To the question "Why not?" she replied, "I don't understand how that can be!" Her words revealed an all too prevalent logic that equates "I don't understand" with "it's not right." Rather than letting the other be (with his/her specific religion, worldview, sexual practices, behavior, etc.), thus creating a more complex picture of our shared world, people persistently demand that others conform to their own standards of behavior or beliefs before acknowledging the presence of another person as an equal in the same society, nation, community, etc.

Expertyza presents an idea of a "common ground" that differs from modern-day notions of identity, solidarity, or cooperation for the sake of a particular goal, which are predominant modes of social organization. Rather, it revives the tradition of the "public realm," as understood and practiced in the ancient Greek polis. Distinct from the private sphere (where questions of survival were managed), the public realm is where a person appears before others — his peers — all equally free in speech and action. Hannah Arendt writes, "The reality of the public realm relies on the simultaneous presence of innumerable perspectives and aspects in which the common world presents itself and for which no common measurement or denominator can ever be devised . . . . Only where things can be seen by many in a variety of aspects without changing their identity, so that those who are gathered around them know they see sameness in utter diversity, can worldly reality truly and reliably appear."[38] TL's documentary theater stages an artificial, temporary public realm that shows us ourselves as cohabitants of a common world. It exposes not only how and about what we speak, but also how we interact with one another, including the inability to speak or listen or establish a connection with the present moment shared by all in the theater.

Politics, as understood and practiced by the ancient Greeks, namely as the process of human speech and action directed at a

---

38   Hannah Arendt, *The Human Condition* (Chicago: University of Chicago Press, 1958), p. 57.

common world beyond the perpetuation of the species, has been all but forgotten in today's world. The ongoing crisis in Ukraine is but one example of the widespread inability of contemporary people to cohabit a common world as seen from their different positions. Over the brief period that Maidan in Kyiv was occupied by protesters, a time characterized by the constant threat of violence and uncertainty about what might happen next, conversations among strangers sprouted up organically out of curiosity toward one's neighbor or the desire to share one's thoughts about what was going on in this incomprehensible situation, often leading to energetic debates on the future of Ukraine, the problems and obstacles it faces. People learned from and about one another as they warmed themselves by makeshift fires, but when attempts were made to organize small groups to articulate common positions or plans of action, this kind of "grassroots politics" did not get very far. After the tragic deaths of over a hundred of those protesters, their public canonization as national heroes, and the return of the square to its previous state, it looks like that brief outpouring of public speech was a localized anomaly.

Today the majority of Ukrainians still demonstrate a culturally conditioned inability to speak: to say with their own words what they themselves think. Formed by a history of Soviet repression—when those who spoke their minds or expressed individual thoughts were liquidated, and those who remained alive were discouraged from any kind of behavior deviating from the norm—they have inherited a culture based on fear and mistrust of the other, as well as an absence of a public space for individual expression. Speech needs to be practiced—it exists only in the moment of enactment, and its potential for endurance depends on its capacity to affect the common world. Unlike society at large, which encourages normalized behavior and modes of expression, TL's documentary theater offers a space for speech as singular public action. According to the project's introductory text, "The theater creates the possibility to begin a conversation. Once you are onstage you are obliged to speak, for silence upholds the words of whoever is speaking. When someone starts speaking, s/he appears, making it possible to defend one's position, to continue the discussion."

In this sense, the participants of any given production of *Ex-pertyza* are "playing at politics." Playing a game means accepting certain rules for the duration of the game as common conventions shared by all participants. Yet it also implies the possibility of "playing around"—experimenting with approaches or tactics allowed by the given situation, or even bending the rules and seeing what happens. Taking part in a production means bearing responsibility for the entire situation, though one can neither predict nor control what will happen: each participant is free to act when and how s/he decides. The "rules of the game" devised by the artists take on an authority that no one involved in the production can claim.

TL's documentary theater has no director; the onstage action progresses without a script or ultimate goal. The conversation is structured around questions written by the participants themselves, related to the topic announced by TL. Discussion begins when anyone on stage picks up and reads one of the questions (lying on the floor and visible to participants and audience alike); likewise, anyone on stage can choose to respond to the given question (though no one must). What happens in the theater (including what does not) depends largely on how participants choose to play the game. It is up to each speaker to decide when to speak and what to say, informed by his/her own sensitivity to the whole situation and perhaps accompanied by reflections on what motivates his/her own speech.

As the architecture of a temporary realized public realm, the rules are not meant to protect any individual from taking offense, getting bored or frustrated, being interrupted or ignored. The documentary theater has no mission to entertain or satisfy the spectator, nor to teach him/her anything or transmit a message; it merely creates conditions that make it possible to see something—a process of establishing a common world (albeit inconclusive and bounded by the time and space of an evening in the theater)—in action, something that is being done not for us but in front of us, even with us. The anxiety that arises when everyone does not know what will happen next produces a tension shared by audience and participants alike.

One of the definitive qualities of the public realm in ancient Greece was its permanence, its ability to withstand the mortality of human life. Such a public realm has long been replaced by contemporary society's devotion to the perpetuation of economic interests and human life. But it makes me think about a different kind of permanence—one that lacks a physical foundation but endures through persistence and repetition. The principle of equality becomes a starting point for any human interaction, where both I and the other person have equal potential to perform a heroic act, equal potential toward evil or good, equal freedom to think and to act, and equal prospects of dying.

Published in a special issue of *Springerin, Kyiv, Moscow and Beyond*, April 2015, pp. 42–45.

Resisting the Temptations of Oblivion

—John, what were you doing in 1943?
—I don't remember.
—1941.
—I was starving in the mud flats of the Steppe.
—1942.
—I was a ghost in the forests of Poland.
—1943...

You may remember the story of John Demjanjuk, or at least his name. He was a Ukrainian-American autoworker from Ohio. In the mid-1970s, his name appeared on a list of possible Nazi collaborators residing in the US, supplied by a Soviet-friendly organization to the US Office of Special Investigations (OSI). In 1986, by then stripped of his US citizenship, Demjanjuk was deported to Israel to stand trial, accused of being the infamously sadistic guard "Ivan the Terrible" at the Treblinka extermination camp. The trial was an international spectacle, staged to honor the victims of the Holocaust. Demjanjuk was convicted in 1988 and sentenced to death. Israel's Supreme Court overturned the conviction in 1993, after evidence surfaced revealing that Ivan the Terrible was actually a different Ukrainian—Ivan Marchenko. Demjanjuk was released from prison and returned to Ohio. (His citizenship would be revoked again, and he'd later be convicted in Germany of being a guard at the Sobibor death camp.) During his trials, Demjanjuk repeatedly denied the accusations but did not provide any evidence to prove his innocence.

The Trials of John Demjanjuk: A Holocaust Cabaret, a play by Jewish-Canadian Jonathan Garfinkel (written in 2004), dances around the silence and speculation about what Demjanjuk was really doing in 1943. The story is told through raucous music, punctuated by dark jokes and uncomfortable ethical questions. Garfinkel's play portrays Demjanjuk as a man with a long personal history irreducible to—but also not detached from—his actions during the war. It follows Demjanjuk's biography from his childhood in Ukraine during the Holodomor,[39] fighting in the Soviet army until

---

39   Holodomor, literally "death by hunger," refers to the man-made famine engineered by Stalin in 1932–1933, which killed around 4 million people in Ukraine.

he was captured by the Nazis and taken as a prisoner of war, and into emigration to the US. The author explained his intention to humanize Demjanjuk in the play as "a way to give specificity to the actions done during the Holocaust by perpetrators; they were done by real people from real places with real lives." We are invited to look at this "ordinary man" as someone who—on another continent, in different circumstances, for reasons we will never know—likely participated in the Nazi project to exterminate the Jews of Europe. By reminding us of the different motivations at play in constructing a publicly visible account of the past (which is always intertwined with individuals' personal histories), a vast space for reflection opens up, where there is no simple option of choosing sides.

Last year, the play debuted in Ukraine, performed by the Misanthrope Theater, following a public scandal that nearly kept the show off the stage in April. I saw it in November at StereoPlaza, a nondescript concert venue in Kyiv. At the outset of the performance, the lights are turned on the audience. "Are there any elderly Nazi criminals in the auditorium who would like to step up and confess to their crimes?" an actor calls from the stage. "No? You know, any one of you is welcome to come onstage and answer for your past." They let us sit with that for a moment. Even in today's era of participatory art, these questions—both serious and slightly absurd—ground us to our chairs. They indicate the gravity of the evening's play, playful as it may be. This is an invitation to look back at that past as one's own and wonder: how will I have to answer for it?

The play embarks on a complex journey, intercutting scenes from Demjanjuk's trial in Israel with scenes from his life and conversations with a sadistic character (perhaps his alter ego?) called Ivan the Terrible. While Garfinkel does include direct quotations from the trials in Israel, the personal conversations and recollections are invented. We see how the pursuit of justice is often mixed with personal ambitions and folly, political motives, and organizational reputations, which turn an individual's life into a public spectacle. In one scene, a bumbling OSI agent conspires with the head of the Israeli War Crimes Unit. Later the star lawyers of Demjanjuk's trial in Israel exchange challenges at adjacent urinals and sing insults at one another in a recurring tune. Even the rusty paperclip, which became a key factor in determining the authenticity of Demjanjuk's Trawniki ID, proving that he trained to be a concentration camp guard, is the subject of a musical number. The play emphasizes how individual deeds are inseparable from large-scale historic events.

"1943" reverberates throughout the evening. I realize suddenly that I began in 1943. It is the year that each of my grandparents left their homeland, Ukraine, setting each of their geographic destinies in motion. In 1943 my yet-unborn-mother's father discovered his name on a "Polish list"[40] and fled Ukraine one night, his wife (my grandmother) following with their young son. 1943 was the year that the Nazis, occupying my other grandmother's village in western Ukraine, decided one day to gather all the teenagers from school and send them to work as slave laborers in Germany. These different events would lead them all to eventually settle in the United States, where my parents would meet . . . and where I would later be born.

Although the play in Kyiv was performed in Russian (translated by Anna Avzan), the lively music and camp delivery of the performers evoke the carefree American culture from which Demjanjuk was wrenched by the ghosts of his Eastern European past. Immigrants like my grandparents saw America—a land unscathed by the battles, bloodshed, and chaos of World War II—as a bastion of safety. We watch John at a baseball game with his son, who is mildly irritated by his father's seriousness. The scene ends with John remarking in awe, "It's not impossible. This is America." In this New World, intentionally oblivious to the past (especially the violent crimes committed by its settlers over the centuries), nothing is impossible, even being divested of citizenship and extradited to Israel to answer for a crime one may or may not have committed over 40 years ago. By telling the story of atrocities committed on the European continent with the casual enthusiasm associated with a land seemingly free of suffering, the "Holocaust Cabaret" begins to bridge the oceanwide and conceptual divide that

---

40   While living in western Ukraine, which had been under Polish rule until 1939, my future grandfather—a member of the patriotic Ukrainian intelligentsia—got wind of the fact that he was a target for murder by Polish insurgents.

allowed so many immigrants to build a "new life" on the illusion that one can leave the past behind (in space, as well as in time).

The play tackles the conflicting desire to be released from what one can't forget and the compulsion to recall what one cannot, or wills oneself not to, remember. It presents the audience with the problem of dealing with the memory carried by those who lived through the war—who committed, suffered, and witnessed atrocious deeds—into the "new" postwar world. Forgetting is often a survival tactic. For all the efforts of survivors to shield their children from the horrors they experienced, memory is transmitted to the next generations. Only they do not know what to do with this inheritance, with these powerful sensations that find no analogous situations in their surroundings to give them meaning. I was the troublesome grandchild who could never reconcile the discordance of my idyllic suburban American childhood and my grandparents' recollections of the war. The boisterous, bordering-on-aggressive performance of the cabaret's musicians and actors awakens my own memories of a past full of shiny surfaces and traces of brutality lurking in the shadows.

There is something about the visceral artistic experience of theater that gives access to the complexity and horror of institutionalized human cruelty like no historical reconstruction or factual account. In a flashback to the Holodomor, when John was a child, his mother intones in a flat voice, "Eat. You need your food. You're a growing boy." As he slowly realizes that the meat he is eating is his beloved dog, Pisha, the entire cast starts howling, moaning different tones of dog suffering. It's a convincing imitation, evincing both laughter and a feeling of horror, disgust, and grief. Later when we hear a cold verbal recollection of the screams of people dying in the gas chambers ("The wails human beings can emit. Like dogs. Only worse"), I remember that howling. There is no need to imitate what cannot be imitated. The imagination feeds off memories of sensations, reconstructing images out of the material of lived experience. Here we are also challenged to make our own connections, not just with the actors imitating howling dogs, but from the dark corners of our own lives.

The "Holocaust Cabaret" raises questions about how we tell the stories of an unspeakably brutal and unimaginable past that will inevitably be repeated if we don't make the effort to try to imagine it. The play creates conditions in which the horrors that I've read about for decades in books and reports suddenly connect with my visceral existence in the present moment. It lets one experience that thin, fragile line between "the good life" (spending an evening entertained at the theater) and dark deeds (past or present). This is done through song and dance, dark humor, raunchy jokes that address the events of this story without timidity or evasion. As the evening progresses, tension builds between the court battle and the increasingly graphic conversations between the "regular fella" John and the murderous camp guard Ivan. We are invited on a tour of the Treblinka death camp as if it were an American county fair. Ivan counts off the statistics from 1943: "248 freight cars of mens' suits exported from Treblinka in one year; 25 freight cars of compressed human hair..." How can one argue that mass murder and jokes, "Holocaust" and "Cabaret," don't mix? All of these things are performed by humans.

This edgy show displays the many layers of right, wrong, suffering, action, victimhood, and perpetratorship that can overlap in the life of a single person. It raises questions about the choices one makes under extreme duress. One begins to imagine oneself in the position of Demjanjuk, a prisoner of war captured by Nazi soldiers, faced with the option of working for them—which means collaboration, which means murder—or risking dying of starvation and exposure as a POW. Do we judge a prisoner's choices by the same criteria as those of a free man? To what extent (if at all) do questions of personal survival justify murder? Garfinkel's play complicates the simple binary of victim and perpetrator, as we begin to see how blurry ethical boundaries become when war is mixed with genocide.

At the show's end, John is alone onstage. He stands up from his wheelchair in silence. The lighting is dim, bluish. He lifts his arms slightly out to the side. Is it a gesture of humble asking forgiveness? Or an invitation to join him? Is it the arrested movement to reach for another and embrace? He bows his head slightly and now—through that magic transformational effect of the theater, which allows concrete things and people to be many things at different times, or all at once—it is I who is standing there onstage, awaiting judgment for crimes I may have committed. John's final silent plea echoes the silence of the actual Demjanjuk, who never spoke about what he really experienced in 1943. In 2011, he was convicted in a second trial in Munich of serving as an accessory to the murder of at least 28,060 Jews as a guard at the Sobibor death camp. He died in Germany in 2012, taking with him the memories of what he did and what he thought.

Garfinkel's play presents the modern audience with the reality of not being able to know what really happened in Demjanjuk's life, yet having to live with the consequences, which we (should) know all too well. It is an invitation to put yourself in Demjanjuk's shoes, to ask yourself (suspending for a moment the urge to immediately judge another), how would you live with your past, the one in which you made choices that led to dire consequences? It asks us to acknowledge that anyone alive today in the Western world is the heir to the deeds committed by their grandparents. I cannot escape where and who I come from. Neither can you. The real difficulty lies in learning to live with these past deeds, to talk about them, to even sing and make jokes about them: whatever is necessary to keep the past in mind. It is only by making that connection with one's own life—including with the gaps in experience, with things I'd never considered before—that we can begin to build tenuous bridges of understanding.

***

Staging a "Holocaust Cabaret" today is a political gesture on many levels. It protests the illusion that we, the heirs of Western civilization, have moved past the atrocities committed by Western civilization less than a hundred years ago. It denies the possibility of breaking with that past through voluntary amnesia. It calls into question the American dream of starting over (one that has been embraced by post-Soviet emerging democracies too), as if from a clean slate, leaving one's history behind and living out only the "good life" promised by economic security.

The Misanthrope Theater's production was scheduled to premiere in Kyiv on April 28, 2017. However, the appearance of the words "Holocaust Cabaret" (with no further explanation) on the marquee of the theater, across from the city's main synagogue, on Holocaust Remembrance Day provoked sharp public criticism from Ukraine's chief rabbi. Within hours of Rabbi Moshe Azman posting a photo to Facebook, Ukrainians and Jews were in an uproar about preventing the "anti-Semitic play" from being shown in Kyiv. The venue where the show was to play quickly backed out of its commitment and a number of other theaters refused their stages for the production. After a press conference with playwright Garfinkel and the Misanthrope's director, Ilya Moshchitsky, the play was ultimately performed at the Vozdvizhenka Arts House, an open-minded, private art gallery completely unsuited for staging a rock-music cabaret before a large audience. To my knowledge, while the scandal surrounding the play's censure was covered widely in the local press, only one review of the performance has been published (in the print-only journal *Ukrainskyi teatr*).

The *Trials of John Demjanjuk: A Holocaust Cabaret* has been performed in Canada, the US, Germany (in 2010, during Demjanjuk's second trial in Munich), and St. Petersburg (after Kyiv, in 2017). Only in Ukraine did the play receive such critical pushback before it was even performed. The response of Kyiv's cultural and religious communities reveals a strong unspoken consensus to leave the ethically ambiguous and violent events of the past beyond public discussion and debate. It also reveals the authoritarian quality of Ukraine's public space, where cultural production, reflection, and discourse are policed by influential individuals in a climate of fearful obedience (or disinterest), repressing memories or topics that might offend or stir dissent. For comparison's sake, the controversial opera *The Death of Klinghoffer* was performed at New York's Metropolitan Opera in 2014, despite months of sharp public criticism and even threats. Hundreds of protesters gathered outside the opera house on opening night, and some tried to disrupt the performance inside the theater. This reflects a robust public sphere, where people passionately disagree, even disturb one another, but persevere in voicing their own positions. Is there even one cultural institution in Ukraine that would stand its ground to do something meaningful but unpopular according to official opinion?

Misanthrope director Moshchitsky crystallized the message of *The Trials of John Demjanjuk* as "the world is very complex." I think that the play was suppressed precisely for this reason, reflecting widespread resistance in Ukrainian society to a complex view of events, whether those depicted in the play, those that happened during World War II, or those that are happening in Ukraine today. Staging the play in Ukraine today raises a number of questions. What responsibility does Ukraine carry for the crimes of individual Ukrainians during the war? How does one judge an individual who was simultaneously a victim of the Nazi regime (as a prisoner of war) and a perpetrator of crimes (as a death camp guard)? What parallels can we draw between the story of Demjanjuk and those of Soviet citizens who would prefer to forget their past deeds, committed under different circumstances but not without consequence?

Could the most disturbing takeaway from the stories of Demjanjuk and of the Holocaust Cabaret in Kyiv be a person's capacity to separate themself from their own deeds, and the ability to justify these deeds by the difficult, seemingly unalterable, circumstances in which they felt compelled to act? By perpetuating these claims, we teach our grandchildren to think themselves incapable of resisting questionable actions, that the situation demands compliance, that there is no choice. This position of helplessness is conveyed with each insistence on historical victimhood. A "Holocaust Cabaret" provokes a person to question the oversimplified schema that pits good people on one side and bad on the other as an adequate model for the complexity of human actions and motives, whether in 1943 or in the present day.

Published in *The Odessa Review*, no. 13 (Spring 2018), pp. 82–86.

Theater on Empire's Edge

Beau Monde on Empire's Edge: State and Stage in Soviet Ukraine *by Mayhill C. Fowler (University of Toronto Press, 2017) details the transformation of the cultural landscape (and theater production and reception, in particular) that took place on the territory of present-day Ukraine from the late Russian Empire, through the Civil War, and into the early decades of the Ukrainian Soviet Socialist Republic. The story, which takes place nearly 100 years ago, resonates remarkably with the challenges Ukrainian artists and cultural actors face today as they struggle to establish adequate conditions for the production and reception of their work in independent Ukraine. At the same time, it provides a much-needed historical foundation from which to analyze the chronic problems in the Ukrainian cultural sphere.*

I moved to Ukraine from the United States after the Orange Revolution. Within a few years, I was engaged in the emerging local contemporary art scene, testing out the ways in which the bonds of community could serve as a substitute for institutions. By 2011, people I had known separately – the artists of the R.E.P. group, performers of TanzLaboratorium, art managers trained at the Soros Center for Contemporary Art, and certain forward-looking curatorial staff members of the National Art Museum of Ukraine – were crossing paths more frequently and working together more closely. Often these collaborations took place informally.

What drew us together was concern for the cultural landscape of Ukraine, an interest in experimental art practices, and a desire to shift modes of presentation and discussion of art away from old-fashioned Soviet customs. We understood that if we didn't exercise our individual agency in public space to talk about and defend our interests, the Ukrainian culture infrastructure would keep serving the ideologically capricious state, the image-conscious oligarchs, or the entertainment industry, but not us – the artists.

It was exciting living in the midst of constant crisis with a small circle of collaborators (some of whom became my closest friends) available at any hour to discuss the issues that troubled me. As long as I had a place to sleep and food to eat, it seemed possible and necessary to maintain a practice of looking, listening, thinking, speaking, and acting in the public sphere indefinitely. But sooner or later the past catches up with you. The conditions in which we were working, which were rooted in events and cultural developments of nearly a century past, proved more powerful than our individual words and actions.

Beau Monde on Empire's Edge: State and Stage in Soviet Ukraine by Mayhill C. Fowler (University of Toronto Press, 2017) reconstructs the historical conditions that shaped the Ukrainian stage, leaving the cultural legacy we encounter today. Based on a decade of meticulous research in documents in Russian, Ukrainian, Polish, and Yiddish, it presents us with the complex and multidimensional story of the formation of the Ukrainian SSR through the interrelated efforts of artists and officials. This history of the theater begins in the borderlands of late imperial Russia (with its many cultural centers) and advances through the early decades of the Ukrainian socialist state, showing how Soviet policies began to centralize political and cultural power in Moscow by the 1930s.

The narrative of this important historical work simultaneously follows the lives of individual actors (the theater director Les Kurbas, playwright Mykola Kulish, and arts official Andrii Khvylia, among others) and the transformation of cultural infrastructure (and policy) as the new Soviet state emerged and solidified its methods for controlling the lives of its citizens. Intricate, semiformal social networks—shaped equally by personal ties and official roles—influenced the creation of artistic works that were more than mere reflections of a particularly tumultuous time; they were invested in shaping the emerging Soviet Ukrainian culture.

Today, to speak of the Ukrainians Kurbas and Kulish as peers of Moscow-based artists such as Solomon Mikhoels and Mikhail Bulgakov requires both acknowledging the bias toward Moscow that prevails in Western scholarship on Soviet culture and elucidating how this perspective was formed. *Beau Monde on Empire's Edge* is a reminder that high-quality art was being produced by people of various ethnicities in multiple languages outside of Moscow in the early decades of the Soviet Union. But it also shows how that work slowly lost status in relation to Moscow, in the process actually becoming less compelling as artistic experimentation gave way to the dictates of state policy.

This project requires reconstructing Ukraine's multiethnic cultural landscape at the turn of the 20th century—where theater was performed in Ukrainian, Yiddish, Polish, and Russian—to demonstrate how those conditions led early Soviet artists and activists to make their decisions while shaping early Soviet cultural policy. Although theater flourished in late imperial Russia in established networks, Fowler notes, "actors, dependent on the whim of fickle audiences and philistine patrons for survival, could be stranded by entrepreneurs and left destitute in a remote village." Early Soviet artists, convinced of the importance of their work to further the socialist project, demanded that the state guarantee their livelihood and provide the resources for enacting their artistic agendas, including audiences. Initially, they were successful: "Kulish, [Ostap] Vyshnia, and Kurbas all depended on state institutions, and all worked with state institutions, to make art." Artists in the Soviet Union enjoyed social prestige, and as long as they were connected with and valued by the state apparatus, they were generously supported—given space in which to rehearse and show their work. These artistic elites were also provided with apartments, often in central and desirable neighborhoods.

As someone who has tried to survive while pursuing artistic work in the 21st century (and Fowler was a professional actress before embarking on her career as a historian), I find the investment of the early Soviet state in cultural production incredible. The production of quality artistic works, considered valuable to the project of developing the new socialist state, was considered more important than the ability to manage allotted resources. The 1920s were a fruitful period for art, theater, and literature in Soviet Ukraine. Artists experimented not only with the forms their work would take when demonstrated before an audience, but with the ways in which that work would be produced. The artists were living and socializing together. The spaces of artistic work, ideological debate, and political and personal life overlapped to a considerable degree, allowing ideas to ferment in an amorphous space.

In 1920s and 1930s Kharkiv, artists, writers, and officials frequented the same cafés and billiard halls, and later inhabited the same residence for writers, Budynok Slovo (House of the Word). Bound by ties both personal and official, and driven to develop a particular Soviet Ukrainian culture through their art and influence, these elites represented the "beau monde" of the book's title. While the term may conjure up images of Parisian cafés and salons, Fowler points out that in the early USSR, "art was discussed in the state apparatus, in state-owned apartments, or in the editorial boards of state-owned newspapers, among other locations frequented by state officials as much as by artists." This aspect of early Soviet Ukrainian culture, where a blurring of official capacities and personal relationships informed public artistic expression, was codified in the interdependent roles of "official artist" and "arts official," a legacy that lives on in Ukraine (and other post-Soviet states) to this very day. Fowler claims, "The structural change of the arts and artists absorbing into officialdom was not imposed by Stalin, but rather resulted from a transformed relationship between artists, officials, and the larger public during the years of civil war and early building of socialism." Her story shows how the zealous desire to create a new culture for Soviet Ukraine produced an all-pervasive state mechanism that destroyed the very people who brought it into being.

This book challenges the debates that pit Ukrainian culture against the Soviet system. According to Fowler, "The beau monde created Ukrainian culture in a Soviet context, and that Soviet layer was not imposed from above, but . . . was part of the mentality of the young elites making early Soviet culture." Ukrainian artists valiantly took on the challenge of creating a culture both Soviet and Ukrainian, and the most fruitful period of cultural production and experimentation in art coincided with ongoing debates on the irresolvable problem of what that "Ukrainian" content might be. The new Ukrainian cultural elites had been elevated to their positions by the revolution and they were deeply invested in the socialist project. Fowler insists that the work (and legacies) of Kurbas, Kulish, and their compatriots must be examined in the context of the early

Soviet Ukrainian project. For her, valorizing these artists without acknowledging their ideological bias means ignoring a very significant aspect — and the revolutionary fervor — of their work.

Arriving in Ukraine after the Orange Revolution, I noticed how much the work of young critical contemporary artists was directly aimed at exposing current social and political conditions with an eye toward change. These artists were using their creative energy and public visibility to make up for the shortcomings of civil society and to help Ukrainian society transition from one ideological system to another. Fowler's description of the tireless men gathered around Mykola Kulish's kitchen table makes me pause:

> "Ostap Vyshnia, who kept his hands in his pockets and complained of rheumatism until Kulish poured him a vodka; Pavlo Tychyna, the lone vegetarian for whom [Kulish's mother-in-law] made onion-filled dumplings; and Mykola Khvyl'ovyi, who smoked non-stop and could never sit peacefully in one place." These men felt "full responsibility for the future of the new art," and believed that it was up to them to make culture for Soviet Ukraine.

I myself remember countless evenings and nights in somebody's Kyiv apartment, sitting around — now with laptops and video cameras — discussing urgent cultural matters (like the appointment of a politician's wife as the director of the National Art Museum, or the dramatic censorship of a contemporary artwork by the director of the Mystetskyi Arsenal) and immediately formulating a collective statement or planning a public action. Why had it never occurred to me, while dealing with the endless stream of urgent problems related to Ukrainian culture, that we were following in the footsteps of the artists of 1920s Kharkiv, where art and life intermixed and work involved both the production of art as well as the construction of the infrastructure to support and display it? I found numerous parallels in this story with my own youthful participation in collective efforts to shape contemporary Ukrainian cultural policy, institutions, and community.

Beau Monde on Empire's Edge maps a transition from desiring, demanding, and creating stable conditions for making and showing artistic work to that of a system where the state and the arts were so deeply intertwined that not only the work produced but also the lives of the artists themselves became accountable to the state. Within a decade, the fervent experimentation of Kharkiv's Literary Fair was subsumed into the excruciatingly organized world of the Soviet Union of the 1930s, with its vast network of informers and interrogators and prison labor camps. It was a world in which an entire artistic or theatrical circle could be executed when one individual fell out of favor with the authorities. Thus, it becomes clear how the desire to radically change the circumstances one was shaped by can produce other no less (or even more) threatening conditions — ones with the power to destroy a career and life, and even obliterate one's historical legacy.

In the early 2010s, it seemed that Ukraine's long official tradition of nurturing ideological art in the service of the state had little to offer as a foundation for a new independent Ukrainian culture that might support and appreciate critical artworks. Members of the local contemporary art community looked further afield, traveling to Europe, reading in English, constructing a hybrid heritage in the international tradition of contemporary art. Without exactly disregarding the past, we didn't peer at it too closely, either. We shared with our early Soviet Ukrainian predecessors an expansive and primarily forward-looking gaze. Kurbas, Kulish, and Khvylovyi looked to their modernist contemporaries in Europe for inspiration for their new Ukrainian socialist art rather than to Moscow and Russia. Theirs was a speculative attempt to create culture both Soviet and Ukrainian, based on dreams for a different future. Could it be that even then, their past caught up to them sooner than they expected — and with tragic results?

"Re-communizing" Soviet Ukrainian theater means reinstating the works and lives of Kurbas, Kulish, and their contemporaries in the context in which they created their works. It means returning to their legacies with the understanding that they were driven by intentions to produce art that would help shape the new Soviet Ukrainian state and bring their socialist dreams to fruition. It also means acknowledging that their stories were first obliterated from memory by the very state that they helped build and only later reconstructed through painstaking scholarly research.

As Fowler's story advances into the 1930s, becoming more complex and convoluted, she comments as a historian on the trickiness of using the transcripts of interrogations as source material. Of course, it is impossible to know who really authored a confession or the degree to which the interrogator or interrogated influenced its formulations. As Fowler has learned through extensive archival research, while testimony given under interrogation cannot be taken at face value, it can offer insight into actual relationships, activities, or even political views. Ultimately, "the documents themselves speak to a certain kind of truth because they reveal the way that officialdom functioned, how they exercised incredible authority over artists' lives, and how connected the secret police was with artists." This heritage is one that we have to contend with today, and this book offers a courageous counterpoint to the Ukrainian state's attempts in recent years to shape "national memory" into something unambiguous and ideologically biased.

Beau Monde on Empire's Edge is a tribute to dreamers, and to those who believe that one's actions can change the world. It is also a story of failure and an unflinching testament to the monsters that dreams can unleash: "That the Soviet state murdered Kurbas and Kulish in November 1937 is a tragedy . . . The tragedy lies not only in the state violence, but also in the failure of the monumental task these artists set before themselves. They aimed to change the theater, and from theater the world—and nothing less." But the book does not end with the tragic deaths in the Gulag of Kurbas, Kulish, and thousands of their fellow Ukrainian revolutionaries and artists (among millions of their fellow Soviet citizens). Fowler carries the story beyond the 1930s, demonstrating how "the culturally rich Russian Imperial Southwest would become the Soviet cultural periphery." As power became more centralized in Moscow, Ukraine's imposed provinciality was emphasized in cultural policy and official decisions that favored stereotyped ethnic tropes over sophisticated work as a reflection of national culture.

Fowler's unique perspective—based on over a decade of scholarly research and a previous acting career—makes *Beau Monde on Empire's Edge* not unlike an evening at the theater. The author invites us to look upon the collection of stories and events that she has so painstakingly arranged as material for invoking personal memories and connecting with our own experiences. The book challenges Ukrainian cultural practitioners and scholars—both subject to the country's weak and dysfunctional infrastructure and working to set up conditions that will be more conducive to critical thinking and artistic reflection in the 21st century—to look hard at this story and interrogate the connections between it and our own endeavors. This requires accepting that our national cultural heroes, who were deeply invested in Ukraine's future, were coauthors of the Soviet project in all its brutality; acknowledging the dangerous power of dreams divorced from memory; and understanding that culture develops gradually—and never from a clean slate. Dancing between biographical sketches, historical narrative, and an analysis of the changing cultural infrastructure from late imperial Russia through the first decades of the Ukrainian SSR, the book demonstrates that history is as much a personal matter and responsibility as something contained in books and official narratives.

Published in *The Odessa Review*, no. 12 (Winter 2017–18), pp. 112–116.

Acknowledgments

Most of this book was written in Ukraine, after Russia's full-scale invasion. My first words of gratitude — along with deep honor and respect — go to the members of the Armed Forces of Ukraine, who work tirelessly, resisting the enemy's attacks and forcing the occupiers out of Ukraine. Thanks to the efforts and sacrifices of the AFU, my fellow Ukrainians and I can keep living at home.

Writing a book is a very solitary endeavor — one that is impossible without the attention, support, and encouragement of MANY!

The brilliant writer Anya Yurchyshyn — my incredibly generous cousin — has been a pillar of moral support and an astute, dedicated editor: without her involvement this book would not be the book that it is.

Maria Sonevytsky — avid Ukraine scholar, musician, writer, and dear friend — has been with me from across the ocean all along: championing my writing from wartime Ukraine; offering practical book advice, close reading, and valuable observations; and sharing familial warmth. I am profoundly grateful for our emotionally charged — and sometimes uncomfortable — discussions about what is happening in Ukraine and how it is perceived abroad, which continue to deepen, broaden, and sharpen my perspective.

Vladislav Davidzon has valued, encouraged, and promoted my writing and reflections on Ukraine's culture since 2017, when he took me on as theater critic of *The Odessa Review*. His lively friendship keeps me on my toes while his talent for audacious public remarks sustains the tradition whereby culture is shaped by individual voices and spirited debate. Thank you, Vlad, for munificently authoring this book's foreword!

Thanks to ibidem Press for bringing this book to the world — to Christoph Ohlwärther for being quick to respond and to Christian Schön for patiently listening to my demands and setting clear limits. This book's fine visuals are the work of talented Ukrainian artists: Lisa Biletska (illustrations) and designer Iryna Derii (map), whose patience and clarity of vision I appreciate and admire!

Andreas Umland, editor of the Ukrainian Voices series, saw the potential for a book in my raw, orthographically inconsistent manuscript and offered a publication contract. *Evergreen Review* editor John Oakes put me in touch with Miracle Jones (a master of dark, unsettling prose), whose enthusiastic response to my first draft got me moving bookward. Talented writer (and Maria's wonderful husband) Franz Nicolay connected me to editor Lynne Ferguson, who magnanimously consulted with me in a moment of crisis and offered to help with proofreading. Graceful and meticulous editor Kerri Cox Sullivan provided subtle, precise copyediting on very short notice, for which I am profoundly grateful.

I've been heartened by pithy correspondence with Askold Melnyczuk — whose rich literary work through writing, translating, teaching, and publishing continually draws attention to the Ukrainian experience — and inspired by the depth and insight his own writings transmit.

Thank you, dear readers of *a Kind of Refugee* on Substack! Your presence and attention on the other side have been an integral part of this endeavor of writing as real-time performance. Whether you're old friends or new acquaintances, your notes and comments (and your donations too!) have nourished me through difficult times.

Katja Kolcio, somatics professor and masterful artist of nuanced, multidisciplinary performances, has brought out the visceral energy of my words. It's been an honor and a pleasure to read my writing via Zoom or in person in artistic collaborations dedicated to sharing Ukraine's rich culture of resistance with North American audiences.

Anna Lazar (who generously welcomed my cat Telepatia into her home indefinitely) has reflected that my writing matters, in particular through her charged translations of several passages into Polish and by organizing a bilingual reading for a wonderful audience in Wroclaw.

Illustrator Bill Brown (Native Cpeaker) and radio host Eric Bond (Talk of Takoma); my high school social studies teacher Dr. Stephen Armstrong; Tess Terrible at Connecticut Public Radio; and intrepid volunteer and performing artist Katya Chizayeva have all broadcast my voice and reflections from Ukraine to their respective communities. Monique Camarra of Eurofile; impassioned Ukrainian writer and scholar Sasha Dovzhyk; visionary NYC artist-activist-archivist Gregory Sholette; and "Substack Reads" have expanded my online readership. Marcel Gascon Barbera, whose captivation with Ukraine is a story in itself, has shared my words and volunteer work with a global Spanish-speaking audience.

Olena Lennon, Kellie Lynch, Michelle Goldhaber, and Moki Kokoris have traveled nontrivial distances to hear me read, to chat in person, and to hug. David Rinaldi, Justin Doughty, Mayhill C. Fowler, Michelle Memran, Dr. Diane Kearney, Monica Eppinger, Alexandra Durbak, Katya Vasilaky, Katie Breen Morin, Marika Kuzma . . . along with dear friends from my hometown and from the vibrant Connecticut Ukrainian diaspora community—thank you for reading and listening and helping me grow!

For my thinking, I am most indebted to Larysa Venediktova. As a mentor, colleague, and friend for well over a decade, she has asked incisive questions and offered generous attention to help me cultivate the capacity to think independently based on what I see and sense. The challenging performances and workshops of TanzLaboratorium, the artistic group she founded, and later Micro-university—a rigorous study group she launched for reading philosophy, practicing dance and mathematics—have provided space for lively, insightful discussions with bright Ukrainian minds. Every conversation I have with Oleksandr Lebediev, my long-time partner in contemplating Ukraine, generates new thoughts. Mariana Matveichuk, Anna Vinogradova, and Olga Komisar are intricately woven into my life story. Mykhailo Ziatin's original thinking, expounded with literary flair, delights and enriches my mind.

My darkest months in Ukraine were brightened by thoughtful correspondence with Marci Shore, whose insightful, elegantly articulated public reflections on Eastern Europe's difficult 20th-century heritage I admire. Writer Wendell Steavenson, for whom I translated in Ukraine, inspired me with her courage, resolve, and brilliant prose. Journalists David Rieff and Ed Vulliamy brought spunk and perspective shaped by decades of war reporting to the table in Kyiv, encouraging me to refine my own position on the significance of Ukraine's fight.

Special thanks to members of my Feldenkrais community — in particular, David Zemach-Bersin, Olena Nitefor, and Seth Dellinger — who have been patient interlocutors as I reimagine how to practice and teach the Feldenkrais Method in Ukraine during the war.

Nothing can substitute for the unadulterated joy of dancing with my friends from the Kyiv Swing Dance Club. This is how I renew my life force.

My enterprising friends in the Ukrainian military, Illia Shpolianskyi and the Zli Ptakhy combat drone unit; Lana Nicole Niland, whose Ukrainian Patriot organization spreads light and love across frontline communities; American veteran volunteers, like Kevin B. Cohen and Christopher Loverro, who've made it their personal mission to help Ukraine make it to victory; my soul sister JoAnn Yurchesyn and the steadfast Ukraine supporters in Vermont — you give me faith that the world is full of more kind, bright, generous spirits than I can see at any given moment.

My sister Natalka and brother-in-law Ryan have provided refuge in their house in the mountains where the air and stars are clearer and sharper than anywhere else I go. Their constancy, curiosity, and gentle intelligence helps keep me sane.

The last word goes to my parents, Lana and Eugene Babij, who have offered tremendous support over the years — including money that would have gone to their grandchildren — while respecting my freedom. They have modeled dedication to family and community, and still cultivate the old American tradition of US citizens influencing their government's agenda through public meetings and civil, persuasive speech. They've also donated thousands of dollars to Ukraine's defense.

UKRAINIAN VOICES

Collected by Andreas Umland

Sergiy Korsunsky, Kobe Gakuin University, Japan

Nadiia Koval, Kyiv School of Economics, Ukraine

Volodymyr Kravchenko, University of Alberta, Edmonton

Oleksiy Kresin, NAS Koretskiy Institute of State and Law, Kyiv

Anatoliy Kruglashov, Fedkovych National University, Chernivtsi

Andrey Kurkov, PEN Ukraine, Kyiv

Ostap Kushnir, Lazarski University, Warsaw

Taras Kuzio, National University of Kyiv-Mohyla Academy

Serhii Kvit, National University of Kyiv-Mohyla Academy

Yuliya Ladygina, The Pennsylvania State University, USA

Yevhen Mahda, Institute of World Policy, Kyiv

Victoria Malko, California State University, Fresno, USA

Yulia Marushevska, Security and Defense Center (SAND), Kyiv

Myroslav Marynovych, Ukrainian Catholic University, Lviv

Oleksandra Matviichuk, Center for Civil Liberties, Kyiv

Mykhailo Minakov, Kennan Institute, Washington, USA

Anton Moiseienko, The Australian National University, Canberra

Alexander Motyl, Rutgers University-Newark, USA

Vlad Mykhnenko, University of Oxford, United Kingdom

Vitalii Ogiienko, Ukrainian Institute of National Remembrance, Kyiv

Olga Onuch, University of Manchester, United Kingdom

Olesya Ostrovska, Museum "Mystetskyi Arsenal," Kyiv

Anna Osypchuk, National University of Kyiv-Mohyla Academy

Oleksandr Pankieiev, University of Alberta, Edmonton

Oleksiy Panych, Publishing House "Dukh i Litera," Kyiv

Valerii Pekar, Kyiv-Mohyla Business School, Ukraine

Yohanan Petrovsky-Shtern, Northwestern University, Chicago

Serhii Plokhy, Harvard University, Cambridge, USA

Andrii Portnov, Viadrina University, Frankfurt-Oder, Germany

Maryna Rabinovych, Kyiv School of Economics, Ukraine

Valentyna Romanova, Institute of Developing Economies, Tokyo

Natalya Ryabinska, Collegium Civitas, Warsaw, Poland

Darya Tsymbalyk, University of Oxford, United Kingdom

Vsevolod Samokhvalov, University of Liege, Belgium

Orest Semotiuk, Franko National University, Lviv

Viktoriya Sereda, NAS Institute of Ethnology, Lviv

Anton Shekhovtsov, University of Vienna, Austria

Andriy Shevchenko, Media Center Ukraine, Kyiv

Oxana Shevel, Tufts University, Medford, USA

Pavlo Shopin, National Pedagogical Dragomanov University, Kyiv

Karina Shyrokykh, Stockholm University, Sweden

Nadja Simon, freelance interpreter, Cologne, Germany

Olena Snigova, NAS Institute for Economics and Forecasting, Kyiv

Ilona Solohub, Analytical Platform "VoxUkraine," Kyiv

Iryna Solonenko, LibMod - Center for Liberal Modernity, Berlin

Galyna Solovei, National University of Kyiv-Mohyla Academy

Sergiy Stelmakh, NAS Institute of World History, Kyiv

Olena Stiazhkina, NAS Institute of the History of Ukraine, Kyiv

Dmitri Stratievski, Osteuropa Zentrum (OEZB), Berlin

Dmytro Stus, National Taras Shevchenko Museum, Kyiv

Frank Sysyn, University of Toronto, Canada

Olha Tokariuk, Center for European Policy Analysis, Washington

Olena Tregub, Independent Anti-Corruption Commission, Kyiv

Hlib Vyshlinsky, Centre for Economic Strategy, Kyiv

Mychailo Wynnyckyj, National University of Kyiv-Mohyla Academy

Yelyzaveta Yasko, NGO "Yellow Blue Strategy," Kyiv

Serhy Yekelchyk, University of Victoria, Canada

Victor Yushchenko, President of Ukraine 2005-2010, Kyiv

Oleksandr Zaitsev, Ukrainian Catholic University, Lviv

Kateryna Zarembo, National University of Kyiv-Mohyla Academy

Yaroslav Zhalilo, National Institute for Strategic Studies, Kyiv

Sergei Zhuk, Ball State University at Muncie, USA

Alina Zubkovych, Nordic Ukraine Forum, Stockholm

Liudmyla Zubrytska, National University of Kyiv-Mohyla Academy

Friends of the Series

ibidem.eu